# THE IRIS QUESTION

Hamish Macdonald

GENERAL EDITOR Jon Nichol

## Contents

| | | |
|---|---|---|
| 1 | Who are the Irish? | 3 |
| 2 | How Britain Became Involved: Anglicisation | 4 |
| 3 | How Britain Became Involved: Plantation | 6 |
| 4 | Revolution and the Act of Union | 8 |
| 5 | Catholic Emancipation | 10 |
| 6 | The Orange and the Green | 12 |
| 7 | The Famine | 14 |
| 8 | Industrialisation | 16 |
| 9 | Discrimination | 17 |
| 10 | The Land Question | 18 |
| 11 | The Fenian Rising | 19 |
| 12 | Home Rule | 20 |
| 13 | Ulster Will Fight | 22 |
| 14 | Ulster Unionism | 24 |
| 15 | Irish Nationalism | 26 |
| 16 | The Easter Rising, 1916 | 28 |
| 17 | Partition | 32 |
| 18 | Civil War to Republic | 34 |
| 19 | The Orange State: A Bloody Beginning | 36 |
| 20 | The Unionists Increase Control, 1922–45 | 38 |
| 21 | Liberal Unionism, 1945–63 | 40 |
| 22 | Catholic Grievances | 42 |
| 23 | Protestant Fears | 44 |
| 24 | Civil Rights | 46 |
| 25 | The Unionist Backlash | 48 |
| 26 | Troops In! | 50 |
| 27 | An Army of Occupation | 52 |
| 28 | Internment, 1971 | 54 |
| 29 | Bloody Sunday | 56 |
| 30 | Power Sharing | 58 |
| 31 | Terror, Priests and Politicians | 60 |
| 32 | Solutions | 62 |
| 33 | The Future? | 64 |

Basil Blackwell

## BLACKWELL HISTORY PROJECT

The First World War
The Second World War
The United States of America
Russia
Modern China
Germany
The Great Power Conflict after 1945
International Relations 1919–39

Agrarian Britain 1700–1900
The Industrial Revolution
Transport 1750–1980
Trade Unions and Social Reform
Social Problems 1760–1980

History of Medicine
The Irish Question
The Middle East
Source Book: How to use Evidence

*'For Marjorie'*

First published 1985

© Hamish Macdonald 1985
Reprinted 1986 (twice)

All rights reserved. No part of this publication may be reproduced, stored in a retrieval system, or transmitted, in any form or by any means, electronic, mechanical, photocopying, recording or otherwise, without the prior permission of Basil Blackwell Ltd.

ISBN 0 631 91440 4

Typesetting by Freeman Graphic, Tonbridge, Kent
Printed in Hong Kong by Wing King Tong Co. Ltd.

## Acknowledgements

BBC Hulton Picture Library 11(G), 14(B), 15(D), 20(E), 29(G), 33(E), 34(E); Belfast Telegraph 38(A), 45(D), 49(D); British Library 28(D); British Museum 23(E); Camera Press cover, 42(E), 50(C), 52(A), 54(C), 56(A), 57(J), 59(E), 63(B), 64(A); The Guardian 64(E); The John Hillelson Agency 64(C); Imperial War Museum 24(C); London Express News and Feature Services 3(B), 25(D), 61(G), 63(D); National Library of Ireland 3(C)(D), 7(F), 8(A), 9(E), 21(G), 26(C), 27(F), 30(J), 32(C); National Museum of Ireland 4(A); Northern Ireland Office 43(G); Popperfoto 10(A), 12(B), 13(F), 41(F), 46(A), 47(D), 51(E), 52(B), 55(G), 60(A), 61(F); Deputy Keeper of the Records, Public Record Office of Northern Ireland 23(F); Punch 3(A), 19(C), 21(F), 33(G); Topham Picture Library 40(D), 48(B).

We are also grateful for permission to use extracts from: *War and an Irish Town* by Eamon McCann, published by Pluto Press (pages 40, 46–47, 48–49, 51, 53, 58); *Across the Barricades* by Joan Lingard, published by Heinemann (pages 58, 64) and *Under Goliath* by Peter Carter, published by Oxford University Press (pages 13, 17).

# 1 Who are the Irish?

Cartoon **A** was drawn in 1882, **B** 100 years later. They both show an English point of view. Is it the same? What view of the Irish do they give? Why? Now look at the Irish cartoons, **C** and **D**. This is how many Irish still see the English. What view do they give?

Who are the Irish? People have been coming to live in Ireland for 2000 years. Around 200 BC bands of Celts were the first settlers. In the ninth century Viking warriors attacked the settlements, and some stayed to build trading towns like Dublin. In 1169 King Henry II of England sent an army to conquer Ireland. Later, English and Scottish Protestants came as settlers. The descendants of all these people now live in modern Ireland.

## ?????????????????

1 Look at cartoons **A–D**:
   a In what ways are they different?
   b In what ways are they the same?
   c Why do you think these attitudes have developed?

2 What clues in **A** and **B** suggest that the English view of the Irish has not changed?

3 a How can you tell that **A–D** are biased?
   b How can biased evidence like this be useful to the historian?

THE IRISH FRANKENSTEIN.

# 2 How Britain Became Involved: Anglicisation

A St Patrick

How did the English become involved in Ireland? The clues on these pages help give the answers.

**A** is a stone carving of St Patrick, the patron Saint of Ireland. At the age of 16 he was kidnapped in England by Gaels (Celts) and brought to Ireland as a slave. He escaped but returned in AD 432 as a priest. Patrick brought the Roman Catholic version of Christianity to Ireland, and it spread quickly.

After Patrick's death in about AD 461 the Gaels began to worship Christ in their own way. By 1100 their religion was different from that of most other Roman Catholics. **B** is a letter of 1155 written by Pope Adrian IV to the Norman King of England, Henry II. In it, the Pope gives King Henry his blessing to invade Ireland in order to restore the Roman Catholic version of Christianity.

*' Adrian, bishop, servant of the servants of God, to our well-beloved son in Christ, the illustrious King of the English, greeting . . . We . . . do hereby declare our will and pleasure that, with a view to enlarging the boundaries of the Church, . . . correcting evil customs and planting virtue, and for the increase of the Christian religion, you shall enter that island and do whatsoever may tend to the honour of God and the welfare of the land . . . '* **(B)**

Pope Adrian IV may have had other reasons for giving his blessing to the English King. He was himself an Englishman — the first to become Pope. Also, control over Ireland would add to the wealth of the Roman Catholic Church. With the Pope's support, King Henry could go ahead with his invasion (see **C**).

The invasion of Ireland was not a success. The Anglo-Norman forces did not get much further than an area around Dublin, called 'the Pale' (see map **D**). Nevertheless, many Normans and English managed to stay on and settle in Ireland. By 1366 the rulers of England were worried that these settlers were getting too friendly with the natives. A law was passed to keep the Anglo-Norman settlers apart from the Gaelic Irish. It was called the Statute of Kilkenny:

*' . . . no alliance by marriage . . . fostering of children (shall) be henceforth made between the English and the Irish . . . that no Englishman or other person . . . shall give or sell to any Irish . . . that every Englishman shall use the English language and be named by an English name . . . and*

## C Timechart

**1155** Pope Adrian IV gave the Norman King, Henry II, his blessing to invade Ireland.

**1169** *1 May* The Earl of Pembroke (nick-named 'Strongbow') sent soldiers to help the Irish King of Leinster, Dermot Macmurrough, in a rebellion. Strongbow later married Macmurrough's daughter, and became King of Leinster when Macmurrough died. Afraid that Strongbow was growing too powerful, Henry II decided to become ruler of Ireland himself.

**1366** The Laws of Kilkenny were passed, to prevent Norman and English settlers mixing with the Irish natives.

**1530s** King Henry VIII changed the religion of England from Roman Catholic to Protestant. He tried to enforce this in Ireland, but met strong opposition. He passed laws to extend English control over Ireland by making the Irish speak English and adopt an English way of life.

*that every Englishman use the English custom, fashion, method of riding and clothes.* (E)

In the 1530s the English tried to extend their control over the Irish. The English King Henry VIII broke away from the Roman Catholic Church and set up his own Protestant Church in England. But most of the Irish remained loyal to the Catholic Church. There was danger of an Irish revolt. Henry VIII made himself King of Ireland and made laws like **F**, passed in 1537:

'*Wherefore be it enacted . . . that no person or persons . . . shall be shaven above the ears, or use any hair covering their upper lips, called . . . a 'cromeal'* (moustache), *or use or wear any shirt, smock, kerchief, . . . or linen cap, coloured or dyed with saffron* (an orange dye).

. . . *And be it enacted that every person shall use the English tongue and language.*

*And further, be it enacted . . . that every person having any house . . . shall keep their houses . . . as near as ever they can, according to the English order, condition, and manner . . .*' (F)

This law tried to *Anglicise* the Irish — to make them become so like the English that they would no longer be England's enemies. But was it possible to turn them all into loyal English Protestants?

## D The invasion of Ireland

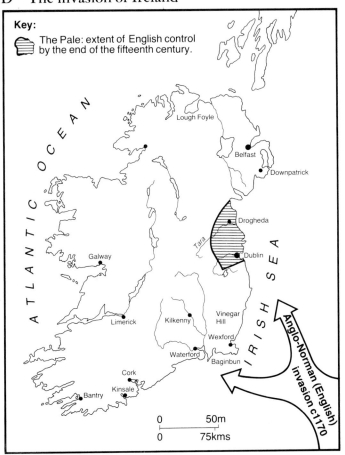

## ??????????????

**1** Is **A** primary or secondary evidence? How useful would it be to the historian?

**2** Which of the following do you think were the real reasons for Pope Adrian IV's interest in Ireland: greed; ambition; wish to spread Roman Catholicism; friendship with Henry II; being English?
Give reasons for your answer.

**3 a** What does Anglicisation mean?
**b** Why did the English rulers make laws like **E** and **F**?
**c** How did the rules in **E** and **F** differ? Why do you think this was?

**4** Imagine you are an Irish Roman Catholic in 1537. How do you feel about: the new laws, Henry VIII, English Protestants? How will Anglicisation affect your life? Will you obey the new laws or fight against them?

**5** In your own words, explain how and why the English became involved in Ireland.

# 3 How Britain Became Involved: Plantation

The unrest in Ireland continued in the reign of Queen Elizabeth I (1558–1603). Many Irish Catholic lords rebelled against Protestantism and English rule. Elizabeth was afraid that Ireland would ally with England's Catholic enemies. Map **A** shows how close Ireland is to England.

Queen Elizabeth was determined to rule Ireland firmly. One of her advisers wrote:

*A barbarous country must first be broken by war before it will be capable of good government.* (**B**)

**C** describes the harsh treatment given to the Irish rebels. One of Elizabeth's deputies ordered:

*. . . that the heads of all those which were killed in the day be cut off from their bodies and brought to the place where he encamped at night, and should be laid on the ground by each side of the way leading to his tent . . . it did bring great terror to the people when they saw the heads of their dead fathers, brothers, children, kinsfolk and friends lie on the ground before their faces.* (**C**)

The Elizabethan attempt to conquer Ireland ended in 1601. To reward her Protestant supporters Elizabeth gave them lands taken from the Catholic Irish rebel leaders. This *plantation* (colonisation) of Ireland by loyal Protestants was taken further by King James I. He began a full-scale plantation of Ulster in 1609, (**D**). Scottish and English Protestants were encouraged to settle on land taken away from Catholics. All they had to do was take an oath of loyalty:

*Every of the said undertakers* (settlers) *shall take the oath of supremacy* (that they were loyal to the King not the Pope) *. . . and shall also conform themselves in religion according to his majesty's laws.* (**E**)

**A** England and Ireland in the seventeenth century

**D** The plantation of Ireland

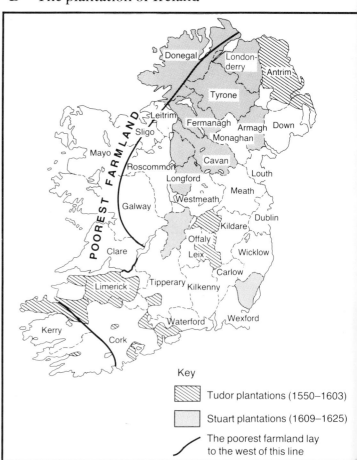

Mrs Fforde's house rifled, and to make her confess where her money lay they took hot tongs, and clapping them to the soles of her feet and to the palms of her hands, so tormented her that with the pain thereof she died.

They have set men and women on hot gridirons to make them confess where their money was.

**F** Extracts from a Protestant account of the Catholic rebellion of 1641

The Protestant settlers soon had reason to live in fear. In 1641 England was split by a Civil War between King Charles I and Parliament. The Catholics in Ireland thought this was a good time to rebel. **F** is a Protestant account of what happened.

By 1649 the English Civil War was over. Oliver Cromwell was sent to Ireland to deal with the Catholic rebellion. The methods he used to crush the rebels were harsh. When English soldiers captured the garrison town of Drogheda they ran wild, killing nearly 3000 people (including 200 women). Afterwards, Cromwell spoke of the massacre as:

*the righteous judgements and mighty works of God.* **(G)**

Cromwell confiscated nearly all the land still owned by Catholics. It was then given to soldiers as payment for their services, and to people who had lent the English Government money. If the Catholics who had lost their land could prove that they had taken no part in the rebellion, they were allowed to take up some of the poor farmland in the west (see **D**).

In 1688 problems in England affected Ireland again. King James II lost the throne of England for wanting to restore the Roman Catholic religion. He turned to King Louis XIV of France, and to Ireland, for support, and war broke out.

In March 1689 King James' army trapped 35 000 Protestants in the city of Londonderry, in Ulster, and laid seige to the city. Robert Lundy, the commander of the garrison, wanted to surrender, but was stopped by the city's Protestant workers. When food began to run out the people ate dogs, cats, mice, candles and leather to stay alive. Thousands died of disease. Still they did not surrender. On 28 July British ships sailed up the river Foyle to the rescue. The siege of Londonderry was over – after 15 weeks.

England had a new Protestant King, who had come from the Netherlands – William of Orange. He was James II's son-in-law. William took his army to Ireland to fight James and his Catholic allies. In 1690 William won great victories at the Battle of the Boyne and at Aughrim. The following year the Catholic armies surrendered.

The Protestants of Ulster still celebrate their victory over the Catholics. Every year in July and August there are *Orange* (after William of Orange) marches and parades through the streets.

# ?????????????

**1 a** What three reasons can you suggest for why the English acted so harshly against the Irish (see **C**)?
**b** What evidence can you find on these pages to support these reasons?

**2 a** What was the purpose of plantation?
**b** Why were the Scottish and English settlers made to swear the oath of loyalty (**E**)?

**3** Tell the story of the events in **F** from the viewpoint of either an Irish Catholic rebel or a Protestant settler.

**4** Why might memories of this period of history divide Catholics and Protestants in Ireland today? (Clues: Elizabethan conquest; plantation; Catholic rebellion; Drogheda; Siege of Londonderry; Battle of the Boyne).

# 4 Revolution and the Act of Union

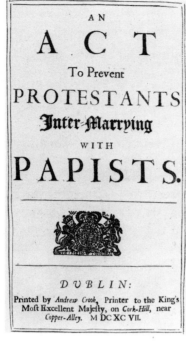 

**A** Two of the penal laws passed against Catholics in Ireland

William of Orange's victories over James II's Catholic armies in 1690 gave Protestants even more power in Ireland. However, there was still a danger of further Catholic rebellion.

Protestants ruled Ireland with a firm hand from their government headquarters and Parliament in Dublin. This Parliament was strictly controlled by the English King. **A** shows the kind of laws passed to weaken the Catholic religion. These *penal* laws, as they were called, also made it impossible for Catholics to buy land and work for the Government:

> *... be it enacted that every person that shall bear any office or offices, civil or military ... in the service or employment of his majesty ... shall take the several oaths of supremacy and allegiance.*
> *... and be it further enacted that all persons that do neglect or refuse to take the said oaths and sacrament shall be adjudged incapable and disabled in law to have the said office or employment.* (B)
>
> (Test Act 1673)

> *And for a further Remedy against the growth of Popery ... be it further enacted that if any Papist shall take upon themselves the Education of Youth in any place within this Realm being thereof lawfully convicted shall be adjudged (sentenced) to perpetual (life) imprisonment.* (C)
>
> (Ban on Catholics teaching, 1700)

Catholics who still owned land mostly had the poorest farmland. Large numbers of Catholics were now tenants or labourers on land which had once belonged to their families. Many Protestant landlords did not live in Ireland. They preferred to be 'absentee landlords' who lived off the profits made from their farms and the rents from their tenants.

Not all Protestants were happy about the way Ireland was ruled. Many English families living in Ireland wanted a much greater say in the running of their own affairs. However, two groups had special reason to grumble: Protestant businessmen, and Protestants who were not members of the Church of England – like the Presbyterians. Irish businessmen were not free to trade with whom they liked; there were laws to protect English businessmen from competition. Protestants who were not Anglicans (members of the Church of England) suffered in the same way as Catholics from laws like the 1673 Test Act.

By 1770 Ireland had much in common with Britain's 13 colonies in America. They too resented being ruled from London and being taxed by the British Parliament. In 1775 the American colonies rebelled and in 1776 declared their independence. During the War of Independence which followed (1776–83) Britain tried unsuccessfully to regain control of her American colonies.

The Irish Protestants were not slow to take advantage of Britain's difficulty. Led by the lawyer Henry Gratton

E An artist's impression of the Battle of Vinegar Hill

(1746–1820) they demanded more freedom to control their own affairs. Britain was afraid the Irish Protestants would copy the Americans and rebel. For this reason in 1782 the Irish Parliament was made more independent.

This did not help those Protestants who were not Anglicans. Wolfe Tone (1763–98), himself an Anglican, sympathised with Presbyterians and Catholics. He wanted all people to be equal and wanted Ireland to be free of *all* control from the British Parliament.

The American revolution and the French revolution in 1789 inspired Wolfe Tone to act. In 1791 he helped set up the Society of United Irishmen. Its purpose was to persuade the parliaments of Britain and Dublin to end the penal laws. Catholics who owned property worth 40 shillings (few did) were given the right to vote in 1793. However, by this time Britain was at war with France and was in no mood to listen to the United Irishmen, especially when Wolfe Tone wrote:

*‘As we well knew what it was to be enslaved, we sympathised with the French people . . .*
*. . . In a little time the French revolution became the political test of every man's political creed (beliefs), and the Nation (Ireland) was fairly divided into two great parties, the Aristocrats and the Democrats . . .’* (D)

Wolfe Tone went to America to avoid arrest. Meanwhile, in 1795, Irish Protestants loyal to Britain formed the Orange Order to protect Anglican Protestants from attack and to keep them in power. The next year Wolfe Tone arrived in France to get support for a rising in Ireland. French ships carrying soldiers tried to land at Bantry Bay but failed because of bad weather.

In May 1798 Wolfe Tone and his supporters began their uprising in Ireland. The loyal Protestants were ready for them. E is a scene from the battle of Vinegar Hill in June 1798. The rebels lost the battle and scattered in confusion. This was the end of the uprising. Government troops continued to hunt and viciously kill the rebels. A Protestant clergyman noted that more than half of the 50 000 who died in the rebellion were killed in cold blood. When Wolfe Tone was captured he slit his throat. He took several hours to die.

The British Government decided it was too dangerous to allow Ireland to continue to have its own Parliament. By an Act of Union in 1800 Ireland was united to Britain. Ireland was to be ruled from the British Parliament. On 1 January 1801 a new flag, the *Union Jack*, was raised over public buildings in Britain and Ireland. Its three crosses symbolise the joining of Scotland, England and Ireland into the United Kingdom of Great Britain.

# ??????????????

**1** How did the penal laws (**A**, **B** and **C**) attack the Catholic religion in Ireland?

**2** Why was the Orange Order founded? Who belonged to it?

**3** Look at **E**. Do you think it gives an accurate picture of the battle, or is it biased in any way? Give reasons for your answer.

**4 a** 'Wolfe Tone was a traitor'
  **b** 'Wolfe Tone was a hero who died for his country'
Use the evidence on these pages to prepare an argument in support of one of these statements. In Northern Ireland today, who might agree with **a**? Who would agree with **b**?

# 5 Catholic Emancipation

**A** A wall painting in the streets of Londonderry

Look at **A**. Today, the population of Northern Ireland is divided over religion. In the whole of Ireland Catholics outnumber Protestants by about four to one. However, most of the Protestants live in the North of Ireland (Ulster). Here, Protestants outnumber Catholics by three to two. Many Irish people belong to religious clubs and societies. These reinforce the division between Catholics and Protestants.

In 1793 Catholics were allowed to vote if they owned or rented property on which they paid 40 shillings tax a year. In Ulster at elections there were fights between rival gangs. After one of these battles at the *Diamond* in Armagh in 1795, the Protestants formed the *Orange Order*. It took its name from King William of Orange (see **A**). To become a member, a Protestant had to swear an oath:

*' I do solemnly and sincerely swear of my own free will and accord that I will to the utmost of my powers support and defend the present King George III and all heirs of the Crown, so long as they support the Protestant ascendancy, the constitution and the laws of these Kingdoms, and I do further swear that I am not, nor ever was, a Roman Catholic, or papist, that I was not, nor ever will be, a United Irishman and that I never took an oath of secrecy to that society. '* (**B**)

Although Catholics could vote they could not become members of parliament. In 1799 William Pitt, the British Prime Minister, let Catholics think that they would be able to become MPs after the Union between the British and Irish Parliaments.

*' ... when the conduct of the Catholics shall be such as to make it safe for the government to admit them to participation of the privileges granted to those of the established religion, and when the temper of the times shall be favourable to such a measure ... it is obvious that such a question may be agitated in a united, imperial parliament, with a much greater safety, than it could in a separate legislature* (parliament). *'* (**C**)

Was this a promise?

After the Act of Union in 1801 King George III refused to allow Catholics the right to become MPs:

*' ... no consideration could ever make me give my consent to what I look upon as the destruction of the established Church which by the wisdom of the Parliament of England I as well as several of my predecessors have been obliged to swear the support of at our coronations ... '* (**D**)

Pitt's words (**C**) now seemed worthless. Voting was done in public. Catholic tenants who voted against their Protestant landlords' wishes could expect immediate eviction. In 1823 a Catholic lawyer called Daniel O'Connell formed the Catholic Association to help tenants and to fight for the right to become MPs.

Daniel O'Connell decided to test the law. In 1828 he stood against a British government minister in an election in County Clare (see **E**). He won enough votes,

G  *Emancipation Pudding; or, Who are the Carvers*

but was refused permission to enter the British Parliament as an MP. This angered Catholics in Ireland so much that the Lord Lieutenant feared there would be trouble:

❛*Such is the extraordinary power of their agitators, that they could lead on the people to open rebellion at a moment's notice, and their organisation is such, that in the hands of desperate and intelligent leaders I believe their success inevitable.*❜ (F)

The Duke of Wellington, who was British Prime Minister, and Home Secretary Robert Peel, wanted to avoid rebellion. They persuaded King George IV and Parliament to pass the Catholic Emancipation Act in 1829, allowing Catholics to enter Parliament as MPs. This upset the Protestants. **G** is a cartoon drawn at the time, showing their reaction. Figure 1 is Daniel O'Connell, 2 is the Pope, 3 is Robert Peel and 4 the Duke of Wellington.

For Daniel O'Connell this was only the beginning. He wanted an end to the Act of Union:

❛*You* (the English) *are unable to govern Ireland even to your own satisfaction; for two-thirds of the time . . . you have ruled her, not by the powers of the law, but by undisguised despotism* (force), *and her misery has been of no advantage to you. In the name of Ireland, I call upon you to do my country justice. I call upon you to restore her national independence*❜ (H)

### E  Timechart: 1823–29

| | |
|---|---|
| 1823 | Daniel O'Connell forms the Catholic Association to campaign for Catholic emancipation. |
| 1824 | With the help of Catholic priests the Association raises money (called Catholic Rent) to pay for the campaign. The money helps tenants evicted for voting against their landlords' wishes. |
| 1826 | The Waterford by-election. A Protestant supporter of Catholic emancipation wins, with the help of the Catholic Association. |
| 1828 | *May* Repeal of the Test Act (see p8). Non-Anglican Protestants can now become MPs, but not Catholics. |
| | *July* Daniel O'Connell wins the by-election in County Clare. He is not allowed to take his place in Parliament because he is a Catholic. |
| 1829 | Fear of rebellion in Ireland forces the British Government to allow Catholic emancipation. |

### ??????????????

**1 a** Why do you think **A** was painted? Who by?
 **b** Why would you expect to find most such wall-paintings in Ulster?

**2** Why did members of the Orange Order have to swear an oath like **B**? What does it tell us about:
 **a** their loyalty to the British King?
 **b** their attitude towards Catholics?

**3** Why did the British government agree to Catholic emancipation?

**4** Look at **G**. What is happening in the cartoon? Do you think it is drawn from a Catholic or a Protestant viewpoint? Why? Draw your own cartoon showing the opposing viewpoint.

# 6 The Orange and the Green

❛. . . *To the glorious, pious and immortal memory of King William III, who saved us from Rogues and Roguery, Slaves and Slavery, Knaves and Knavery, Popes and Popery . . . and whoever denies this toast may he be slammed, crammed and jammed into the muzzle of the great gun of Athlone, and the gun fired into the Pope's belly, and the Pope into the Devil's Belly, and the Devil into Hell, and the door locked and the key in an Orangeman's pocket.*❜ **(A)**

A is a toast used by the Orange Order in the early nineteenth century. Orange parades and marches caused serious riots in 1849, 1857, 1886 and 1969. Each year the Protestant orders march through Northern Ireland towns with their sashes, banners, bands and pounding drums (B). As they march past the homes of Catholics they sing old Protestant fighting songs like the *Boyne* and the *Sash* and new ones like:

**B**   A Protestant Orange parade through Belfast

❛*If guns were made for shooting,
Then skulls are made to crack.
You've never seen a better Taig (Catholic)
Than with a bullet in his back . . .*❜ **(C)**

and

❛*Slaughter, slaughter, holy water,
Slaughter the Papists one by one.
We will tear them asunder
And make them lie under
The Protestant boys who follow the drum.*❜ **(D)**

The Catholics have their own parades and marches. Instead of orange they use green for the colour of their sashes and ribbons. They have clubs and societies like the Ancient Order of Hibernians, to match the Protestant Orange Order. Catholics too sing songs, which are full of hatred and violence towards Protestants:

*'Oh St Patrick's Day will be jolly and gay,
And we will kick all the Protestants out of the way.
If that won't do
We'll cut them in two
And send them to hell with their
Red, white and blue.'* (E)

The events of the past continue to play a large part in forming the ideas of both Protestants and Catholics. Protestants remind Catholics of the victories of William of Orange in the 1690s; Catholics remember the uprisings of their heroes like Wolfe Tone in 1798 (see page 9).

Religious beliefs underlie the hatred in Northern Ireland today. Church leaders do not always work for peace between Irish Catholics and Protestants. In 1857 riots were sparked off in Belfast by an open air meeting held by the Protestant Reverend Hugh 'Roaring' Hanna. Another Protestant leader, the Reverend Ian Paisley (F) became famous in the 1960s for his anti-Catholic speeches and protests. In one, he described a group of Catholics as:

*'Blaspheming, cursing, spitting, Roman Scum.'* (G)

and he called the Pope

*'The scarlet whore (prostitute) of Rome.'* (H)

On 14 July 1969 the *Irish Times* reported a speech made by Paisley:

*'I want to say that I am an anti-Roman Catholic as far as the system of Popery is concerned . . . But God being my judge I love the poor dupes (fools) who are ground down under that system.'* (J)

Do people always join the Protestant and Catholic bands, marches and parades for religious reasons?

*Under Goliath* by Peter Carter is a story about two boys growing up in Belfast. Alan, a Protestant, joins Mr Mackracken's drum and fife band. His main reason for joining is that he wants to bang a big drum called 'the lambeg':

*'Now there is what you might call a drum: five feet across and three wide, made from the skins of a dozen lambs stretched on a wide circle of oak, painted with the heads of heroes, and bound with silver struts. When you pound on that you use canes four feet long, and as it throbs the panes in your windows rattle, pots fall off the shelf, doors shake, and the false teeth clatter in old men's heads. It has a call that would stop your heart from beating – and maybe your mind from thinking.'* (K)

Across the park from the Orange Lodge where Alan practises is a Catholic Church hall. There Feargus Riley, a Catholic, plays the bagpipes in a Catholic band. The

**F** Dr Ian Paisley

two boys meet, call each other names and fight, but eventually they become friends! When Feargus takes Alan to his home Alan is surprised by what he sees:

*'I sat back and had a good look at the house. It was the same as ours but it wasn't papered as nicely. It was full of religious pictures too . . . There was a crucifix on the door and a picture of Jesus pointing at his heart, and one of Jesus as a baby, and over the fireplace there was a big picture of the Pope. But what amazed me was that over the Pope there were pot ducks exactly like in our house . . .'* (L)

Why was Alan surprised? What else might he find that he and Feargus had in common? Why is it unusual in Northern Ireland for boys like Alan and Feargus to become friends?

---

# ??????????????

**1** What does evidence **A–D** tell us about the beliefs of the Orange Order today?

**2** Why do you think Ian Paisley hates the Pope?

**3** Why do Protestants and Catholics sing songs like **C**, **D** and **E** in their parades? What effect do you think these songs have:
  **a** on the people who hear them?
  **b** on the people who sing them?

**4 a** What was Alan's real reason for wanting to join Mr Mackracken's band (**K**)?
  **b** Why do you think Alan was surprised by what he saw in Feargus Riley's house (**L**)?

**5 a** How reliable is evidence **K** and **L**? Give reasons for your answer.
  **b** In what ways can novels like *Under Goliath* be useful to historians?

# 7 The Famine

Disaster! In 1846 there was a total failure of the potato crop in Ireland. A traveller reported:

*‹On coming down from the mountain I rode into the lowland country and there I found . . . the leaves of the potatoes on many fields withered and a strange stench filled the atmosphere adjoining each field of potatoes . . .›* (A)

Ireland was a land of peasant farmers. They and their animals lived almost entirely on potatoes. All the corn and other food they produced was used to pay rent to the landlords. Without potatoes, the peasant farmers were forced either to eat their corn and other food, or starve. Many were unable to pay their rents, and were evicted from their farms (B).

Hunger made people desperate:

*‹There have been attacks on flour mills in Clonmel by people whose bones protruded through the skin which covered them (and with) staring hollow eyes . . .›* (C)

D shows a riot in a potato store.

When all the food was gone, thousands began to die of starvation and disease. This eye-witness report appeared in *The Times* on Christmas Eve, 1846:

*‹In the first (house), six famished and ghastly skeletons, to all appearances dead, were huddled in a corner on some filthy straw, their sole covering which seemed a ragged horsecloth, their wretched legs hanging about, naked above the knees. I approached with horror, and found by a low moaning they were alive – they were in fever, four children, a woman and what had once been a man . . . in a few minutes I was surrounded by at least 200 such phantoms, such frightful spectres as no words can describe, either from famine or from fever. Their demoniac (devilish) yells are still ringing in my ears, and their horrible images are fixed upon my brain . . . The same morning the police opened a house on the adjoining lands, which was observed shut for many days, and two dead corpses were found, lying upon the mud floor, half eaten by rats.›* (E)

The British people were shocked by what was happening in Ireland. Even before the worst failure of the crop, the British Prime Minister, Robert Peel, urged

**B** Poor tenants being evicted from their farm

**D** An attack on a potato store during starvation riots in Galway

**G**

Parliament to take action:

*'Are you to hesitate in averting famine which may come, because it possibly may not come? Or, Good God, are you to sit in cabinet and consider how much diarrhoea and bloody flux, and dysentry, a people can bear before it becomes necessary for you to provide them with food?'* (**F**)

But too little was done too late. A million people died in the potato famine.

Others – over a million of them – tried to escape misery and death by emigrating, (**G**). About 75 per cent of the emigrants went to the United States (mainly New York) and others to Canada. But conditions in the ships were so bad that many did not survive to reach their destination. One emigrant ship, the *Loosthawk*, took seven weeks to cross the Atlantic. When it arrived at Quebec, a third of its 348 passengers had died.

Many Irish people felt that the Famine could have been avoided, like the reformer James Fintan Lalor, who said:

*'A people whose land and lives are . . . in the keeping and custody of others, instead of their own, are not in a position of common safety. The Irish famine of '46 is example and proof. The corn crops were sufficient to feed the island. But the landlords would have their rents in spite of the famine, and in defiance of fever. They took the whole harvest and left hunger to those who raised it. Had the people of Ireland been the landlords of Ireland, not a single human creature would have died of hunger.'* (**H**)

Was Fintan Lalor right? Would things have been different had the 'people of Ireland been the landlords of Ireland'?

# ?????????????

**1 a** Why was the potato so important to most Irish people?
**b** How do you think the Famine is remembered today by: Protestants; Catholics?

**2** Look at **B**. What do you think the artist thought about the evictions? Give reasons for your answer.

**3** Look at cartoon **G**.
   **a** What does it show?
   **b** Is it an accurate picture of a real Irishman?
   **c** What does the cartoon suggest about the artist's attitude towards the Irish?

**4** *Either* Imagine you are an MP who has just listened to Peel's speech (**F**). Write a short speech you would make in the debate, either supporting or opposing British aid for Ireland.
*Or* Write the words for a ballad or song which might have been written to keep alive memories of the famine.

# 8 Industrialisation

From 1800 an Industrial Revolution took place in Ireland. The main industrial growth was in Protestant Ulster. Ulster became richer than the rest of Ireland, thanks mainly to its textile and shipbuilding industries. In Belfast, Ulster's capital, in 1852, there was only one power loom in the linen industry. By 1862 there were 6000 and by 1900, 31 000. In 1842 the total tonnage of ships built in Ireland per year was 1000 tons. By 1914 it was 256 547 tons. Altogether 22 000 men were employed in the Belfast shipbuilding yards in 1914. Most of today's industries are still those set up from 1800–1900, (**A**).

Ulster in 1911 had 1 in 2 of all the industrial jobs in Ireland. Belfast alone employed 1 in 5 of all Ireland's industrial workers. The growth of industry meant that many people went to live in the towns in Ulster. Separate Catholic and Protestant areas grew up in places like Belfast and Londonderry. These *ghettoes* were cut off from one another, causing the towns and cities to be divided into two communities. Competition for jobs increased the tension. For example, in Belfast there were riots in 1886. **B** is part of an official report:

‘*The town is of very recent growth and the result is that the poorer classes . . . reside* (live) *mainly in separate quarters . . . given up to persons of one particular faith, and the boundaries are sharply defined. In the district of West Belfast, the Shanklin Road is an almost purely Protestant district . . . The great Catholic quarter is due south of the Shankill district and (is) known as the Falls Road . . . The great points of danger to the peace of the town are open spaces in the border land between the two quarters; and two of these spaces . . . the Brickfields and Springfield . . . have been the theatres of some of the worst scenes of the riots.*’ (**B**)

In Belfast today, a quarter of the population is Catholic. **C** shows how the city is split into Catholic and Protestant areas.

A  Main industries in Ulster

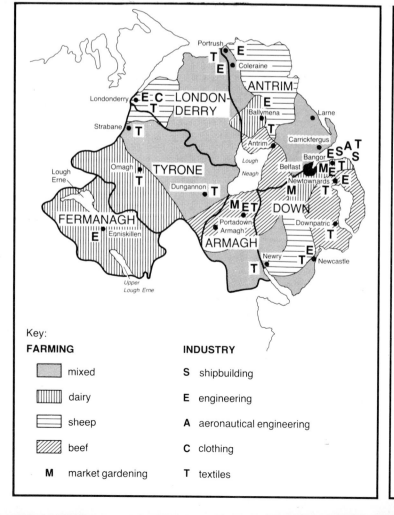

Key:
**FARMING**
- mixed
- dairy
- sheep
- beef
- M  market gardening

**INDUSTRY**
- S  shipbuilding
- E  engineering
- A  aeronautical engineering
- C  clothing
- T  textiles

C  How Belfast is divided

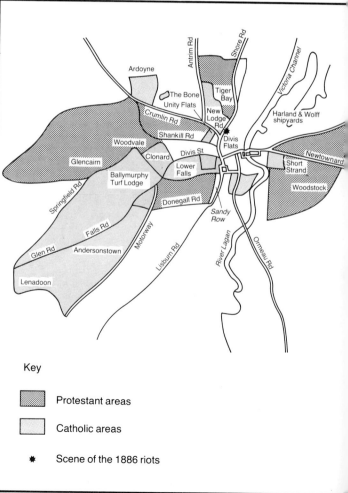

Key
- Protestant areas
- Catholic areas
- ∗  Scene of the 1886 riots

# 9 Discrimination

## Candidate A

**for the job of council recreation officer**
*Name:*   Timothy Duffy.
*Education:*   Belfast College of Technology, University of Loughborough, Ulster College, Northern Ireland Polytechnic.
*Examinations passed:*   National examination board in supervisory management, diploma in supervisory management, recreation management certificate, diploma in management studies, 3rd, 2nd and 1st class certificates in turf culture and sports ground management.
*Member of:*   British Institute of Management; Institute of Supervisory Management; Association of Recreation Managers (chairman of Northern Ireland branch); Institute of Groundsmanship.
*Experience:*   Assistant recreation tourist officer.

**He didn't get the job: he's a Catholic**

## Candidate B

**for the same job: recreation officer**
*Name:*   William Morton.
*Education:*   Left school at 14.
*Examinations passed:*   None.
*Member of:*   Institute of Groundsmanship; Northern Ireland Industrial Safety Group.
*Experience:*   Gardener; landscape supervisor.

**He got the job: he's a Protestant**

C   Discrimination in Employment 1981

Protestants owned most of the industries in Ulster. They feared that Catholics from the rest of Ireland might move to Ulster and soon out-number them. The Orange Order encouraged Protestant employers to discriminate against Catholics. In 1933 Sir John Davison, the Grand Master of the Orange Order, said:

❛*It is time Protestant employers of Northern Ireland realised that whenever a Roman Catholic is brought into their employment, it means one Protestant vote less . . . and I suggest the slogan should be: Protestants employ Protestants.*❜ (A)

How seriously did Protestant employers take this advice? Even in recent times Catholics have found it more difficult to get jobs than Protestants. **B** and **C** came from an investigation made by the *Sunday Times* newspaper:

❛*But the big employers of labour were privately run companies, and although Catholics regularly suspected anti-Catholic prejudice among foremen or personnel managers, it is a hard thing to prove. All that can be recorded is that of 10 000 workers in the Belfast shipyard – the biggest single source of employment in the city – just 400 are Catholic . . .*❜ (B)

D is from a report on employment in Northern Ireland:

❛*The main points which have emerged from this examination of the 1971 Northern Ireland population census can be outlined as follows: Unemployment is experienced at a much higher level by Roman Catholics than by Protestants . . .*
*. . . there was a tendency for those industries which had the highest weekly manual wage in 1971 to be predominantly Protestant, a tendency which was still more marked for women . . .*❜ (D)

In the story, *Under Goliath*, Goliath is the giant crane in the Belfast dockyard where Alan's father and brother, Billy, work. Alan is a Protestant. At first he cannot understand why there are people in Belfast who do not share his pride in the building of Goliath:

❛*It was something, standing under a great crane and looking at the huge dock. It made me proud to see it because it was in Belfast, and I was a Belfast lad, and because Dad and Billy worked in the same yard as Goliath. In fact everyone in Belfast was proud of Goliath . . . It showed that Belfast wasn't just a worn out old city full of slums but, like our Billy said, a city full of skills.*
*But, I must say, I did think it was strange that while the men worked building Goliath and the new dock . . . away across the river other men were creeping about in the night blowing up the reservoirs and burning post offices, just destroying things . . .*❜ (E)

It is not until he gets to know Feargus Riley, a Catholic, that he begins to understand.

## ??????????????

**1 a** What are the main industries in Ulster today?
**b** How did industrialisation make Ulster different from the rest of Ireland?
**c** Why were many Irish people attracted to towns and cities in Ulster from the countryside and from Southern Ireland?

**2 a** Why have separate Protestant and Catholic areas grown up in towns and cities like Belfast and Londonderry?
**b** Suggest two reasons why there were riots in Belfast in 1886.

**3** What evidence is there that Protestant employers still discriminate against Catholics?

# 10 The Land Question

70 per cent of Ireland is farmland. But in 1870 only 3 per cent of the population were landowners. The question of who should own the land caused great bitterness. Hatred of the landlords was aggravated by the fact that most of them were descended from Scottish and English Protestants who had settled on land taken away from the Catholics. The Catholics lived as tenants – but they felt they had more right to the land than their landlords. James Finton Lalor (1807–49) campaigned for their rights:

*'The principle I state is this, that the entire ownership of Ireland is vested of right in the people of Ireland; that they, and none but they, are the landowners and law-makers of this island.'* (A)

The population of Ireland grew rapidly in the early nineteenth century. This meant more mouths to feed, and more hardship for poor peasant families. Landlords demanded high rents, and if the tenants could not pay they were evicted.

The potato famine of the 1840s (see pages 14–15) nearly halved the population. But it did not help solve the land question (see B). The evictions went on, and bitterness towards landlords increased:

*'... almost my first-remembered experience of my own life and of the existence of landlordism was our eviction in 1852, when I was about five years of age ...'* (C)

Towards the end of the 1870s Irish farmers had two severe blows. The first was competition from North America, which began to send cheap corn to Europe. The farmers had to lower their prices to compete – and the small Irish tenant farmers were soon unable to pay their rents. Then, in 1877, bad weather destroyed the potato crop.

In 1879 Michael Davitt (who wrote C) set up the Land League to campaign for lower rents and protection against evictions. The Land League forced politicians to take notice of the suffering of the tenant farmers. The politicians began to think that they could put a stop to unrest in Ireland if they solved the land question.

The British Government put controls on the power of landlords, (D). By the end of the nineteenth century many Protestant landlords were selling off their land. The British Government lent tenants the money to buy some of the land for themselves. By 1916 almost 64 per cent of the population owned land.

The land question was settled at last, and the bitterness died down. But had the Irish question been solved, as the British Government hoped – or had it simply become a different question?

### B  The land question

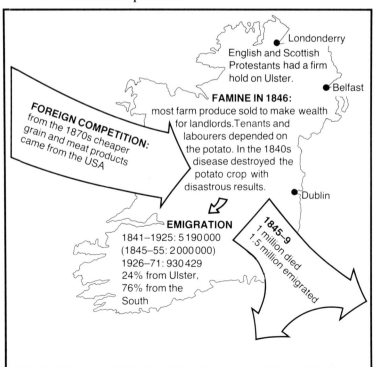

### D  Timechart: How the British Government Helped Tenants to Buy Land

| | |
|---|---|
| 1881 | **Land Act:** set up a Land Court and Land Commission to fix fair rents and to lend tenants money to buy land. |
| 1885 | **Ashbourne Act:** gave the Land Commission five million pounds to lend tenants. |
| 1891 | Land Commission lent thirty million pounds to tenants who wanted to become landowners. The Congested Districts Board was set up to help start new industries and help tenants buy land, or improve it. |
| 1903 | **Wyndham Act:** made a hundred million pounds available to 252 400 tenants – they could borrow this money in order to buy the land they were renting. |
| 1909 | **Birrell Act:** a further 66 500 tenants became landowners. |

# 11 The Fenian Rising

'*... in the presence of God, to renounce all allegiance to the Queen of England, and to take arms and fight at a moment's warning to make Ireland an Independent Democratic Republic, and to yield obedience to the commanders and superiors of this society.*' **(A)**

**A** is part of an oath sworn by members of the Irish Republican Brotherhood – the *Fenians* – in Dublin in 1858. The Fenians were Irish Nationalists – they wanted Ireland to be a united country, free from foreign control, and they were willing to back a revolution.

After the potato famine, some Irish Nationalists had talked of using force to win freedom from British rule. By 1858 the movement had gained strength, and the revolutionaries in Ireland and America formed themselves into the Fenians. By 1865 they claimed to have 85 000 men in Ireland ready to fight.

In 1867 the Fenians rose against the British (see **B**). But they were betrayed by one of their own men, called Corydon. He told the British Government of their plans. The rising failed, and the Fenian leaders were arrested and sent to prison in England.

In September 1867 two of the Fenian leaders – called Kelly and Deasy – were being taken away from Manchester police court in a police van, on their way to prison. Suddenly the van was ambushed by about 30

THE FENIAN GUY FAWKES.
**C** 'The Fenian Guy Fawkes'

armed Fenians. In the struggle one of the police sergeants was shot dead. Kelly and Deasy were set free and escaped. They were never recaptured. But later three Irishmen were arrested. They had been present at the ambush, and were tried for murdering the policeman. They were all found guilty and executed. The three became national heroes. They were known as the Manchester Martyrs.

Later in 1867 there was another Fenian attack. This time they were trying to rescue one of their leaders, Richard O'Sullivan Burke, from Clerkenwell Prison in London. The attack failed, but 30 people were killed and many others badly injured. **C** suggests what many British people thought of the Fenians.

**B  Timechart: The Fenian Rising**

| | |
|---|---|
| 1840s | *Potato Famine* killed 1 million people and forced over 1½ million to emigrate. Many went to America. |
| 1858 | Revolutionary Irish Nationalists formed the *Fenians* (Irish Republican Brotherhood) in Ireland and America. |
| 1866–1867 | *Fenian Rising* They planned to start uprisings at the same time in different parts of the country. The rising began with an arms raid on Chester Castle in England. Corydon betrayed the plans. *September* A police sergeant was killed during an attack on a police van in Manchester to release two Fenian leaders. Three Irishmen were arrested and executed – the 'Manchester Martyrs'. A bomb explosion during a raid on Clerkenwell Prison to rescue a Fenian leader killed 30 people. |

## ??????????????

**1** Why was the question of who owned the land no longer such a source of bitterness by the 1920s?

**2** What was the artist of cartoon **C** trying to say about the Fenians?

**3** Write a letter as a supporter of the Fenians, arguing against the decision to hang the three 'Manchester Martyrs'.

# 12 Home Rule

William Gladstone was the leader of the British Liberal Party. When he became Prime Minister of Britain in 1868 he said:

❛My mission is to pacify Ireland.❜ (A)

Gladstone thought that there were two main causes of the Fenian troubles: the land question (see page 18) and the 'church question'.

The official religion of Ireland was Protestant. The majority of Irish people were Roman Catholic. Catholics had to pay taxes to pay for the building and upkeep of Protestant churches.

Many Catholics bitterly resented paying for an alien church. So, in 1868, Gladstone ended compulsory payment of church rates (taxes) and in 1869 *disestablished* the Church of Ireland. This meant that Protestantism was no longer the official religion, paid for by government taxes.

The next year Gladstone passed a Land Act to protect tenants against unfair eviction by their landlords.

Irish Nationalists like the Fenians were not satisfied with Gladstone's efforts. Many Catholic and Protestant Irish people wanted to run Irish affairs themselves. They wanted their own Parliament in Dublin, which would be in charge of Irish *home affairs*. This was called Home Rule.

In 1870 the Home Rule Association was formed:

❛Home Rule would give (us) the right of making laws for controlling all matters to do with the internal affairs of Ireland, while leaving to the Imperial Parliament the power of dealing with all questions affecting the imperial crown and government (i.e. foreign affairs).❜ (B)

The Home Rule Association was a political party. It aimed to get its supporters elected as MPs in the British Parliament in London, where they could fight for Home Rule. The party soon had enough MPs to defeat the Government if it voted with the opposition.

Protestants as well as Catholics supported the Home Rule Party. In 1877 a Protestant landlord, Charles Stewart Parnell, became leader of the Party. Parnell wanted more than Home Rule: he wanted complete independence:

❛When we have undermined English misgovernment, we have paved the way for Ireland to take her place among the nations of the earth. And let us not forget that it is the ultimate goal at which all we Irishmen aim . . . None of us, whether we are in America or Ireland, or wherever we may be, will be satisfied until we have destroyed the last link which keeps Ireland bound to England.❜ (C)

Parnell and the Irish MPs tried to disrupt the running of Parliament. They made long speeches, heckled and interrupted other speakers. While this behaviour won publicity and gained support from the

E  Protestors 'boycotting' a load of turf

Catholics, Parnell's action in Ireland frightened away many Irish Protestants who had supported the party.

Gladstone's Land Act had failed to solve the land question. Parnell took the side of tenants against their landlords. In 1879 he became Chairman of the Irish National Land League. This is the advice he gave to tenants at a big outdoor meeting at Ennis in 1880:

*Now what are you to do with a tenant who bids for a farm from which his neighbour has been evicted . . . You must show what you think of him on the roadside when you meet him, you must show him in the streets of the town, you must show him at the shop counter . . . even in the house of worship, by leaving him severely alone, by putting him into a sort of moral coventry, by isolating him from the rest of his kind as if he were a leper of old, you must show him your detestation of the crime he has committed.* (**D**)

In 1880 a retired army officer, Captain Boycott, who was agent for the absentee landlord Lord Erne, was driven from the country after this kind of treatment. This gave the English language a new word – 'boycott'. Cartoon **E** shows how Parnell's advice was put into practice.

Parnell's campaign was a major threat to Gladstone. **F** shows Gladstone struggling against the Land League. He decided to take action against Parnell, and in 1881 had him arrested and sent to prison. Gladstone also passed another Land Act, to fix fair rents for tenants and give them better protection against unfair eviction than

**F** This cartoon shows William Gladstone fighting the 'Irish Devil-fish'

**G** Gladstone (seated) being threatened by the Land League

the first Land Act had. He hoped this would improve relations between landlords and tenants.

In February 1882 Gladstone released Parnell from prison. Many people were against this, (**G**). William Forster, the Chief Secretary for Ireland (the British government minister in charge of Ireland) resigned in protest. In his place Gladstone appointed Lord Frederick Cavendish. On the evening he arrived in Dublin to start his new job, Lord Cavendish and his under-secretary were ambushed and murdered. The killers belonged to a secret society called *The Invincibles*. They had once been members of the Irish Republican Brotherhood.

Gladstone knew that his attempts to 'pacify' Ireland had failed. What was he to do now?

# ??????????????

**1 a** What did William Gladstone mean when he said *'My mission is to pacify Ireland'* (**A**)?
   **b** How did he try to solve the Irish question?
   **c** How successful was he?

**2 a** What does *boycott* mean?
   **b** What do you think is happening in cartoon **E**?

**3** Look at **F**:
   **a** What does the cartoon show?
   **b** What message do you think the artist was trying to put across?
   **c** How useful are cartoons **E**, **F** and **G** as historical evidence?

**4 a** What was Home Rule (**B**)?
   **b** How does source **C** show that Parnell wanted more than Home Rule?

# 13 Ulster Will Fight

Growing support in Parliament for Home Rule worried Irish Protestants. They were loyal to England and did not want to see an end to the Act of Union which had joined Great Britain and Ireland in 1800. In May 1885 the Irish Loyal and Patriotic Union (ILPU) – the Unionists – was formed to elect MPs who supported the Union and opposed Home Rule. The ILPU was based in Protestant Ulster.

The Home Rule Party did much better than the Unionists in Ireland in the General Election in November 1885. In fact they did so well that the Conservatives or Liberals needed their support if either wanted to form the next government (see **A**).

**A  Number of Seats won in the House of Commons**

| Conservatives | 249 (only 18 of whom were Irish Unionists) |
| Liberals | 335 |
| Irish Nationalists | 86 (The Home Rule Party in Ireland held 85 seats) |
| | 670 |

**D** 'Lord Randolph Churchill leads on the Demon of religious strife to do the work of Hell in the North of Ireland'

Gladstone decided to support Home Rule. He now believed that this could solve the Irish Question. He also wanted the Liberals to form the next Government. The Unionists were determined to stop him.

Encouraged by the Orange Order the Unionists became a political party in January 1886. They turned to English Conservatives like Randolph Churchill to help them stop Home Rule. His slogan was:

‘*Ulster will fight, Ulster will be right!*’ **(B)**

Churchill's plan was to use the Orange Order to help unite the Protestants in Ulster against Home Rule:

‘*I decided some time ago that if GOM (Grand Old Man – a nickname for Gladstone) went for Home Rule the Orange Card would be the one to play.*’ **(C)**

Cartoon **D** shows what one newspaper thought of this plan. To Churchill and to several members of Gladstone's Liberal Party there was more at stake than just Ireland. Home Rule might inspire Nationalists in other parts of the British Empire to follow Ireland's example.

Gladstone asked the House of Commons to agree to a law for Home Rule in Ireland in April 1886. The opposition was well organised – in June, Home Rule was rejected by 343 to 313 votes (93 Liberals voted against the bill). Cartoon **E** is a comment on this defeat for Gladstone. Look at the background of the picture. It shows a riot.

In Ulster the hard winter of 1885–6 meant distress and higher unemployment for both Catholics and Protestants. The Orange Order and politicians stirred up hatred and discrimination against Catholics.

Trouble broke out in the Belfast docks on the 3 and 4 June 1886. A Protestant mob ran wild. The army was called in to restore order. Fighting continued to break out in Belfast and in other towns through the rest of the summer. 32 people were killed, 442 arrested and 377 policemen were injured.

Soon after this the Home Rule Party was weakened by a scandal. In 1890 its leader, Parnell, was taken to court in a divorce case by the husband of his mistress, Mrs Katherine O'Shea. Roman Catholic supporters were horrified when Parnell refused to resign as leader of the Party. When Parnell died in October 1891, at the age of 45, he left the Home Rule Party bitterly divided.

Parnell's death did not stop Gladstone. In 1893 his second Home Rule Bill was passed in the House of

Commons but was defeated in the House of Lords which had the power to reject laws.

The Home Rule Party was reunited in 1900 under the leadership of John Redmond. By 1911 the Liberals had enough support in Parliament to reduce the power of the Lords to stop Bills becoming Acts (laws). The House of Lords could now only delay bills for two years. In 1912 another Home Rule Bill was introduced. Despite defeat in the Lords it was due to become law in 1914.

The Unionists, led now by Edward Carson, were furious and prepared to resist Home Rule in Ulster. On Saturday, 28 September 1912 about 450 000 men and women signed a document (**F**) called 'Ulster's Solemn League and Covenant'. Some signed with their own blood.

Bonar Law, the leader of the Conservative Party, declared his support for the Unionists. In January 1913 the Ulster Volunteer Force was formed to resist Home Rule by force.

**E** A cartoon commenting on the defeat of Gladstone's Home Rule Bill

## Ulster's Solemn League and Covenant

Being convinced in our consciences that Home Rule would be disastrous to the material well-being of Ulster as well as of the whole of Ireland, subversive of our civil and religious freedom, destructive of our citizenship and perilous to the unity of the Empire, we, whose names are underwritten, men of Ulster, loyal subjects of His Gracious Majesty King George V., humbly relying on the God whom our fathers in days of stress and trial confidently trusted, do hereby pledge ourselves in solemn Covenant throughout this our time of threatened calamity to stand by one another in defending for ourselves and our children our cherished position of equal citizenship in the United Kingdom and in using all means which may be found necessary to defeat the present conspiracy to set up a Home Rule Parliament in Ireland. And in the event of such a Parliament being forced upon us we further solemnly and mutually pledge ourselves to refuse to recognise its authority. In sure confidence that God will defend the right we hereto subscribe our names. And further, we individually declare that we have not already signed this Covenant.

The above was signed by me at Belfast "Ulster Day." Saturday, 28th September, 1912.

*Edward Carson*

### God Save the King.

**F** Ulster's 'Solemn League and Covenant'

# ?????????????

**1** What did Protestants have to fear from the results of the General Election in 1885 (**A**)?

**2 a** Why did Randolph Churchill encourage Ulster to fight Home Rule (**B**)?
**b** What did Churchill mean by 'the Orange Card' (**C**)?
**c** What is happening in **D**?
**d** What was the Ulster Volunteer Force?

**3** Do you think **E** is sympathetic or unsympathetic to Gladstone? Give reasons for your answer.

**4** List the reasons why the Liberals were unable to pass the Home Rule bill until 1912.

**5** Draw up a document like the Solemn League and Covenant (**F**) to be signed by Catholics in favour of Home Rule.

# 14 Ulster Unionism

Why would Ulster fight? Ulster covers 26.3 per cent of Ireland. The biggest plantation of Protestants took place here in the seventeenth century. Today two-thirds of the people of Ulster are Protestant and own most of the land and businesses.

In 1914 most Protestants wanted Ireland to remain united with Great Britain under the Act of Union of 1800. In a united independent Ireland Roman Catholics would outnumber them and be able to outvote them. The Protestants feared that an Irish Home Rule Parliament would pass laws to allow the Catholic Church to interfere with how their children were educated, how they worshipped, and to take away some of their rights to free speech.

Unionists thought Home Rule for the whole of Ireland would result in a united independent Ireland. To fight against Home Rule was not enough. The Unionist leaders prepared to make Ulster independent of both Ireland and Great Britain (see A). In March 1914 the Liberal Government suggested that the British army would be used to force the Unionists to accept Home Rule. 58 officers stationed at the Curragh Camp in Ireland resigned in protest. Large amounts of money were raised to buy guns from Germany to arm the Ulster Volunteer Force. Yet Ulster Unionists were still loyal to the King of England. This loyalty was put to the test when England went to war with Germany and Austria in August 1914. To win the Unionists' support it was agreed to delay Home Rule until the war was over. The Unionist leader, Edward Carson, told his supporters:

‘*England's difficulty is not Ulster's opportunity.*’ (B)

He sent 35 000 UVF members to fight with the British Army.

C shows men from the 36th (Ulster) Division resting in a trench on 1 July 1916, during the Battle of the Somme. 5500 Ulstermen died in this battle. The West Belfast Battalion, 'The Shankill Boys' lost 630 out of 700 men. Unionists still talk of their sacrifice for 'King and Empire'. This meant that the British Government was unable to force Ulster to join an all-Ireland Republic after the First World War.

A  The proclamation of provisional government in Ulster

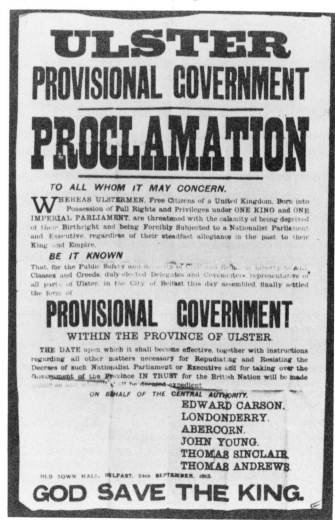

C  Soldiers from Ulster in the trenches

# THE NEW STANDARD

*Incorporating the* **Evening News**

Friday, February 6, 1981.    Price 12p.

**CLOSING PRICES**

## 500 men pledge to die rather than see Ireland united

# PAISLEY'S ARMY ON PARADE

'This is only a small token of the many thousands of men who are pledged to me...'

*Ian Paisley*

IAN PAISLEY paraded 500 men from a private Protestant army on a windswept Ulster mountain today and vowed they were "ready to fight and die rather than accept an all-Ireland Republic."

**D** Headlines from the London *New Standard* newspaper, 6 February 1981

---

Today Ulster is still part of the United Kingdom. Protestant leaders like Ian Paisley, whose father was a member of the UVF, are still prepared to fight against Independence (D). In the newspaper article, Paisley was:

'... asked the significance of the waving of firearms certificates ... he said 'It means that these men hold guns legally and they are prepared to defend their province and their rights in the same way as Lord Carson and the men of the Ulster Volunteer Force were prepared'.' **(E)**

---

## ??????????????

**1 a** What reason is given in **A** for the decision of Ulster Unionists to form their own government?
 **b** Why was it agreed to delay Home Rule until the First World War was over?
 **c** Why was it difficult for the British Government to force Ulster to join an all-Ireland Republic after 1918?

**2** What might the officer of the men in **C** say in 1916 about:
 **a** his reasons for fighting?
 **b** his ideas on the Home Rule Bill?
 **c** his thoughts about the Curragh mutiny?
 **d** his hopes for the future?

**3** How do **D** and **E** show that history both explains and causes division in Ireland today?

25

# 15 Irish Nationalism

A  Timechart

| | |
|---|---|
| 1884 | Nationalists formed the Gaelic Athletic Association to revive Gaelic sports like Gaelic football and hurling. It encouraged local patriotism and a strong dislike of foreign games. |
| 1893 | The Gaelic League was formed to keep alive Gaelic as the Irish national language and to encourage the Irish to speak, read and write in it. |
| 1905 | Arthur Griffith formed a new Nationalist Party called Sinn Fein to work for complete independence for Ireland by peaceful methods. |
| 1913 | *January* Irish Nationalists formed the Irish Volunteers to fight for Home Rule. *November* Workers on strike in Dublin formed the Irish Citizen Army to defend themselves against the police. |
| 1914 | *August* Britain declared war on Germany. |

For the Nationalists Home Rule was not enough (see A). Nationalist leaders like Arthur Griffith wanted Ireland to be:

*'A self governing land, living, . . . moving and having its being in its own language . . .'* (B)

Griffith wanted to have nothing to do with Great Britain. In 1905 he helped form a new political party – *Sinn Fein*. 'Sinn Fein' is Gaelic for 'Ourselves'. Its plan was to use peaceful methods to win independence for Ireland. Sinn Fein would take part in elections but its MPs would not sit in the English Parliament at Westminster. Instead they planned to set up their own Parliament in Ireland and ask the people of Ireland to obey only the laws made by this Parliament.

At first, few nationalists had faith in this plan. Many saw Home Rule as a step towards independence. Others thought of revolution as the answer. There were also those who believed that Socialism and trade unions could help.

High unemployment and low wages in Dublin led trade union leaders like James Larkin (C) and James Connolly to urge workers to unite and strike:

*'Why use one arm when we have two? Why not strike the enemy with both arms – the political and the economic?'* (D)

In 1913 a strike in Dublin by workers on the tramways caused employers to join together to lock out all members of Larkin's Irish Transport Union. The strike lasted six months. There were riots when the police used baton charges to break up crowds who had come to listen to Larkin. An eye-witness said:

*'I saw them baton an old woman with a shawl over her head and attack a small man who had lost his hat . . . There was continual rapping of batons on people's heads . . . you could hear from the cries and shrieks that the same thing was happening opposite the metropole and opposite the Post Office.'* (E)

In November 1913 the strikers formed the Irish Citizen Army to defend themselves against the police. F shows their Dublin headquarters. The strike failed, but the bitterness it caused united the working-classes of Dublin against the employers and slum landlords. At that time 87 000 people – almost a third of Dublin's population – lived in miserable slums. Often, families had only one room, without heat, light, sanitation or water, except for a shared tap in the passage or yard. Disease spread quickly in such conditions, and Dublin had the highest death rate in the country.

Several of these slum landlords and employers belonged to the Home Rule Party. This was one reason why many working-class nationalists turned to other

C  James Larkin

**F** Members of the Irish Citizen Army outside their Dublin headquarters

forms of nationalism. Some agreed with James Connolly that:

*The struggle for Irish freedom has two aspects: it is national and it is social. The national ideal can never be realised until Ireland stands forth before the world as a nation, free and independent. It is social and economic because no matter what the form of government may be, as long as one class owns as private property the land and instruments of labour (jobs), that class will always have it in their power to plunder and enslave the remainder of their fellow creatures.* (**G**)

However, it became clear in 1913 that the Protestants of Ulster were prepared to fight to resist Home Rule (see pages 22–23). Nationalists of all kinds joined the Nationalist armed force – the Irish Volunteers. Both the Irish Volunteers and the Irish Citizen Army were prepared to fight for Home Rule.

The threat of Civil War between Irish Nationalists and Protestants in Ulster was lifted by the outbreak of the First World War in 1914. John Redmond, leader of the Home Rule Party, agreed to wait for Home Rule until after the war:

*I have come here tonight to join with the responses of all parties, and all creeds, and all classes . . . in Ireland to tell . . . the people of Great Britain that Ireland has in full a heartfelt sympathy with the objects of this war . . .* (**H**)

Many Nationalists followed Redmond's call to fight for England against Germany. But a number agreed with James Connolly when he said:

*We have no foreign enemy except the treacherous government of England – a government that even whilst it is calling us to die for it, refuses to give a straight answer to our demand for Home Rule.* (**J**)

## ??????????????

**1 a** Why did Arthur Griffith want Ireland to have its own language (**B**)?
  **b** What was Sinn Fein's plan to win independence for Ireland?
  **c** Why was the Irish Citizen Army formed?
  **d** Why did James Connolly call the British Government a 'foreign enemy' (**J**)?
  **e** What does the slogan above the Irish Citizen Army's headquarters mean (**F**)?

**2** For what reasons did John Redmond decide to support Great Britain in the First World War? What effect did this have on the fight for Home Rule?

# 16 The Easter Rising 1916

D  Newspaper headlines announcing the capture of Sir Roger Casement

Every year Irish Republicans visit the grave of Wolfe Tone (see pages 8–9) at Bodenstown to pay their respects. In June 1913 a schoolmaster and Gaelic League poet, Patrick Pearse, said:

'We have come here not merely to salute this noble dust and pay our homage to the noble spirit of Tone. We have come to express once more our full acceptance of the gospel of Irish Nationalism which he was the first to formulate . . . To complete the work of Tone . . . we need not re-state our programme; Tone has stated it for us: "To break the connection with England the never failing source of all our evils"' (A)

That year Pearse joined the Irish Republican Brotherhood. He was prepared to die in a 'blood sacrifice' to win independence for Ireland:

'Ireland will not find Christ's peace until she has taken Christ's sword . . . We must not faint at the sight of blood. Winning through it, we (or those of us who survive) shall come unto great joy.' (B)

Pearse was among those in the Irish Volunteers (formed in 1913) who did not wish to fight for England in the war with Germany in 1914. Another member, Sean Kelly, wrote:

'. . . three weeks after the war had started a meeting was held at which it was decided that Ireland should make use of the opportunity of the European war to rise in insurrection (rebellion) against England. There were eight or nine people at that meeting including Tom Clarke, Patrick Pearse, Sean MacDermott, Eamonn Kent, Arthur Griffith, William O'Brien, Sean McGarry, a man called Toblin, and myself.' (C)

Together with the Irish Citizen Army led by James Connolly, they planned to take over Dublin at Easter in 1916.

Their plans went wrong. A week before Easter the British Navy captured a German ship carrying 20 000 rifles and ammunition for the rebels. There were a number of arrests including that of Sir Roger Casement (D) who had persuaded the Germans to send arms. Despite the fact that the British Government now had warning of their plans for an uprising, Pearse and Connolly decided to go ahead.

On Easter Monday 1916 about 1600 men took up their positions in different parts of Dublin, ready for attack. About 100 of them marched to the General Post Office in Sackville street (see map H). Firing revolvers into the air they took over the Post Office and made it their headquarters. Moments later Patrick Pearse declared that Ireland was now an Independent Republic.

When the rising began the rebels were outnumbered by British troops by about three to one. Within 48 hours British troops outnumbered the rebels by twenty to one. Still more troops poured into the city. It seems that the rebel leaders knew they were not strong enough to win. Connolly had said:

'We are going out to be slaughtered.' (E)

Nevertheless, it was not an easy fight for the British troops. Many of them had been trained in the trenches, and were not used to the guerilla tactics used by the rebels.

There was a week of fierce street fighting. The British army fired two 18-pounder guns at close range in the streets, while the gunboat *Helga* fired shells from the

F  An artist's impression of the scene inside the Dublin GPO

G  British troops in the ruins of the GPO after the Rising

river Liffey. The damage was enormous. Fire almost completely destroyed Sackville Street. **F** is an artist's version of the scene inside the rebel headquarters, the General Post Office. The man on the stretcher is James Connolly. Though shot twice, once in the ankle, he continued to command his soldiers to the end. **G** shows British troops examining the remains of the General Post Office after the Rising had been crushed.

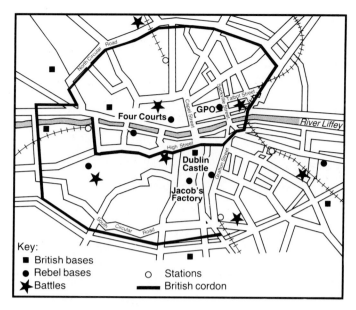

**H** Dublin during the Easter Rising

Map **H** shows where the main events of the Rising took place. Both the Volunteers and the British Army were ruthless. They shot many people in cold blood, including unarmed civilians. One such incident involved a civilian called Francis Sheehy Skeffington. He went into Dublin to try to help the wounded and stop his fellow citizens from looting and wrecking shops. But as he returned home on 25 April he was arrested by an Army officer, Captain J.C. Bowen-Colthurst. Skeffington was held as a hostage and taken out on a raiding party, where he saw Bowen-Colthurst shoot an unarmed youth. The next day he and two journalists were taken out and executed, without a trial. Later, it was proved that Bowen-Colthurst was mad, he was put on trial and found guilty of murder. On 19 April 1916 the rebel leaders surrendered (**J**). 300 civilians, 60 rebels and 130 British soldiers had died in the fighting. Over 2000 were injured.

Chart **K** outlines the course of the rising. Was it worth it? Pearse had said:

**J** The rebels' surrender note

> In order to prevent the further slaughter of Dublin citizens, and in the hope of saving the lives of our followers now surrounded and hopelessly outnumbered, the members of the Provisional Government present at Head-Quarters have agreed to an unconditional surrender, and the Commandants of the various districts in the City and Country will order their commands to lay down arms.
>
> P. H. Pearse
> 29th April 1916
> 3.45 p.m.
>
> I agree to these conditions for the men only under my own command in the Moore Street District and for the men in the Stephen's Green Command.
>
> James Connolly
> April 29/16
>
> On consultation with Commandant Ceannt and other officers I have decided to agree to unconditional surrender also.
>
> Thomas MacDonagh

**K** Timechart: The Easter Rising

**1914**  *4 August*  Britain enters the First World War.
*18 September*  The Home Rule Act is passed, but Home Rule is delayed until after the war.
*20 September*  John Redmond, the Home Rule Nationalist leader, urges the Irish Volunteers to support Britain in the war. This splits the Irish Volunteers. The majority, re-named National Volunteers, join the British Army to fight; a small number (members of the IRB and Sinn Fein) keep the name Irish Volunteers and refuse to fight. Instead they plan a rebellion against British rule in Ireland.
*15 October*  Sir Roger Casement, an Irish Nationalist who had worked for the British Government, goes to Germany to get arms and men to help the Irish rebels.

**1915**  *May*  The Irish Republican Brotherhood (IRB) set up a military committee to plan the rising. One of its members is Patrick Pearse. By the end of the year the date for the Rising has been fixed for Easter 1916.

**1916**  *January*  James Connolly, leader of the Irish Citizen Army, joins the IRB military committee.
*February*  The rebels tell the Germans that the Rising is to take place on 23 April.

*'Well, when we are all wiped out, people will blame us for everything, condemn us; but (if it had not been) for this protest the war would have ended and nothing would have been done. After a few years, they will see the meaning of what we tried to do.'* (L)

At first most people in Dublin were shocked and angry. As they were led away to prison the rebels were spat at and threatened by hostile crowds.

But soon the public attitude changed. The Catholic Irish were horrified when they heard that 77 rebels had been sentenced to death. In the end only 15 were executed. These included Patrick Pearse and the other leaders. James Connolly had to be strapped into a chair before being shot because he was too badly injured to stand. The Home Rule MP, John Dillon, warned the British Government:

*'You are letting loose a river of blood . . . between two races who, after 300 years of hatred and strife, we had nearly succeeded in bringing together.'* (M)

He also said:

*'. . . the great bulk of the population were not favourable to the insurrection (rising) . . . They got no popular support whatever. What is happening is that thousands of people in Dublin, who ten days ago were bitterly opposed to the whole of the Sinn Fein movement, and to the rebellion, are now becoming infuriated against the government on account of these executions, and, as I am informed by letters received this morning, that feeling is spreading throughout the country in a most dangerous degree . . .'* (N)

The leaders of the Easter Rising in 1916 were added to the list of Republican martyrs (see also pages 9 and 19). Today their example is admired and remembered (see page 43). Republicans continue to make 'blood sacrifices'. In 1981 Republicans in the Maze H-block prison in Northern Ireland went on hunger strike. They wanted to be treated as political prisoners and not as criminals, and wanted to wear their own clothes instead of prison uniform. When their demands were refused, ten of the men starved themselves to death.

---

*21 April* Casement arrives in Ireland to warn the rebels that the Germans are sending only arms, not men. He is arrested soon after landing, and later hanged for treason.

*22 April* The British Navy intercepts the German ship the *Aud* which is carrying arms to the rebels. The German crew sink the ship to prevent it being captured.

*23 April* Eoin MacNeill, official leader of the Irish Volunteers, tries to call off the Rising, but it is too late.

*24 April* (Monday) The Rising begins with an attack on Dublin Castle. The rebels take over the General Post Office as their headquarters.

*25 April* Fierce fighting in the streets. The British Army use heavy artillery at close range.

*26 April* Murder of pacifist Sheehy-Skeffington. Gunboat *Helga* shells rebel targets from the River Liffey.

*27 April* Dublin GPO catches fire, forcing the rebel leaders to move their headquarters to a fishmonger's shop in Great Britain Street.

*29 April* The rebels surrender.

*3–12 May* Rebel leaders executed by firing squad.

---

# ??????????????

**1 a** Why did Patrick Pearse believe that 'blood sacrifice' would help win independence for Ireland?

**b** Why does the newspaper headline in **D** describe Sir Roger Casement as an 'Irish traitor'?

**c** What did the leaders of the Uprising think they would achieve (**E**, **L**)?

**d** How far does evidence **M** and **N** support Pearse's beliefs in **L**?

**2** As if you were a newspaper reporter, describe the scene in **F**. Explain where you are, what is happening and what the fighting is about. Mention what you can see in the picture.

**3** Compare **F** and **G**

**a** Which details in **G** match the details in **F**?

**b** What message is the artist of **F** trying to get across?

**c** How reliable is **F** as a source of evidence?

**4** Write a short play about the murder of Francis Sheehy Skeffington. Include: the outbreak of fighting in April 1916; looting in the streets; helping the wounded; the arrest; the shooting of the unarmed youth; the murder of Skeffington and the journalists; Bowen-Colthurst's trial.

# 17 Partition

After 1916 support for Sinn Fein grew. Many Irish people were sickened by the execution of the rebel leaders (see page 31).

In November 1918 the First World War ended. In December there was a general election in Britain. Sinn Fein's election manifesto said:

*'... Sinn Fein aims at securing the establishment of* (the Irish) *Republic:*
*1 By withdrawing the Irish representation* (MPs) *from the British Parliament and by denying the right and opposing the will of the British government or any other foreign government to legislate* (make laws) *for Ireland.*
*2 By making use of any and every means available to render impotent* (make useless) *the power of England to hold Ireland in subjection by military force or otherwise.*

**B    Timechart: Events leading up to Partition**

| | | |
|---|---|---|
| 1918 | *December* | British General Election. Sinn Fein won 73 out of 105 Irish seats. Sinn Fein MPs refused to attend the British Parliament. They formed their own Parliament – Dail Eireann. |
| 1919 | *January* | Dail Eirann declared Ireland to be an Independent Republic. The British Government refused to accept it. Start of the War of Independence: Michael Collins led the Irish Republican Army in attacks on the police in Ireland. |
| 1920 | *March* | British ex-soldiers – the Black and Tans – volunteered to help the police fight the Republicans. |
| | *July* | British ex-officers – the Auxillaries – arrived to help the police and Black and Tans. |
| | *December* | Auxillaries and Black and Tans burned down the centre of Cork in revenge for IRA killings. The Government of Ireland Act partitioned Ireland into two. The North agreed to accept Home Rule. The South refused anything short of complete independence. The Anglo–Irish Treaty ended the fighting. Southern Ireland remained part of the British Commonwealth and became the Irish Free State. |

C   A police 'wanted' poster for the arrest of Daniel Breen

*3 By the establishment of a constituent assembly* (Parliament) *comprising persons chosen by Irish constituencies as the supreme national authority to speak and act in the name of the Irish people, and to develop Ireland's social, political and industrial life, for the welfare of the whole people of Ireland ...'* (A)

Sinn Fein won 73 out of 105 seats in Ireland. The Unionists won 26. The Home Rule Party won only six. The Sinn Fein MPs refused to go to the British Parliament in London. Instead they set up their own Parliament in Dublin, called Dail Eireann. On 21 January 1919 they declared Ireland to be an Independent Republic (see **B**). The British Government refused to accept this.

On 21 January 1919 Daniel Breen and Sean Treacy (see **C**) ambushed and killed two policemen escorting a cart of gelignite to a quarry at Soloheadbeg, Co. Tipperary. Breen later wrote:

*It is our proud claim for Soloheadbeg, that it was the first deliberate planned action by . . . the Irish Volunteers renewing the armed struggle, temporarily suspended, after Easter Week 1916 . . .* **(D)**

The Irish Republican Army (IRA) was formed, led by Michael Collins. In 1919 they began attacks on police and soldiers working for the British. This was the start of a War of Independence. By the middle of 1920, 200 members of the Royal Irish Constabulary (RIC) were resigning every month because of threats and intimidation.

The British Government recruited ex-soldiers to restore its authority in Ireland. They were known as the 'Black and Tans' because of their khaki uniforms and dark green police belts and hats. **E** shows Black and Tans in action. They became famous for their lack of discipline and acts of terror. There was also a force of ex-army officers called the Auxillaries, better paid than the Black and Tans but just as ruthless.

Protestant Unionists backed Britain in the war against the Nationalists. In Ulster, Protestant mobs attacked Catholics. In one attack at Lisburn in 1920, 273 homes were burnt out. One man recorded in his diary:

*It reminded me of a French town after it had been bombarded by the Germans as I saw in France in 1916. We visited the ruins of the Priest's house on Chapel Hill. It was burnt or gutted and the furniture all destroyed . . .* **(F)**

**E** The Black and Tans in action

THE KINDEST CUT OF ALL.

**G** A cartoon commenting on Lloyd George's plans for the Partition of Ireland

Britain's Prime Minister, Lloyd George, decided there was only one way to stop the war (**G**). In 1920 his government passed the Government of Ireland Act. It aimed to restore peace by a temporary *partition* of Ireland: to divide Ireland into two countries, each to have Home Rule but to be separate. A Council of Ireland, with members from North and South, would be set up to work out how to reunite Ireland peacefully. The six North-Eastern counties of Ulster formed one country. Southern Ireland, consisting of the remaining 26 counties, was the other. Though not entirely happy, the Unionists accepted Home Rule in the six counties of Ulster. But the Nationalists continued to fight for a United Independent Ireland.

# ??????????????????

**1** How did Sinn Fein act to make Ireland independent between November 1918 and 21 January 1919?

**2 a** Why did the British Government bring in the Black and Tans and the Auxillaries to keep law and order?
**b** What does **E** suggest about their methods?

**3** Design an IRA 'Wanted' poster like **C**, for the capture of members of the Black and Tans or Auxillaries.

# 18 Civil War to Republic

E  Armed anti-treaty Republicans marching through Dublin

In the War of Independence Irish Nationalists killed 600 and wounded 1200 people who fought on the British side. The British forces killed 752 IRA men and wounded 866. By 1921 some of the Nationalist leaders, including Michael Collins and Arthur Griffith, were ready to sign the Peace Treaty which the British Government now offered:

*Ireland shall have the same constitutional status in the community of nations known as the British Empire as the Dominion of Canada . . .*

*The oath to be taken by members of the parliament of the Irish Free State shall be in the following form:*

*I, . . ., do solemnly swear true faith and allegiance to the constitution of the Irish Free State as by law established and that I will be faithful to His Majesty King George V, his heirs and successors . . .*

*The government of the Irish Free State shall afford to his majesty's imperial forces . . . in time of war or of strained relations with a foreign power such harbour and other facilities as the British Government may require for the purposes of defence.* (A)

Who had won – the Nationalists or the British? As Michael Collins signed the Treaty in London he said:

*I am signing my death warrant.* (B)

But when they arrived back in Dublin Arthur Griffith argued:

*. . . it is the first treaty that admits the equality of Ireland . . . we have brought back the evacuation of Ireland after 700 years by British troops . . .* (C)

Many Nationalists were furious. The President of the Dail, Eamon de Valera, pleaded:

*I am once more asking you to reject the Treaty for two main reasons . . . it gives away Irish Independence; it brings us into the British Empire; it . . . acknowledges the head of the British Empire . . . as the direct monarch of Ireland, as the sources of executive (governing) authority in Ireland.* (D)

The Dail voted to accept the Treaty by 64 votes to 57. But the Anti-Treaty Republicans (E) were determined to wreck it. Eamon de Valera supported them. Soon the Nationalists were fighting one another in a Civil War (see F). Disappointed and exhausted by overwork Arthur Griffith died of a heart attack on 12 August 1922.

At 7.30 pm on 22 August, Anti-Treaty Republicans ambushed Michael Collins as his armoured car stopped in front of obstacles which they had placed across the road. According to one historian:

*It was later said, and is still sometimes believed in Ireland even today, that he had been shot by one of his own side, either by the machine-gunner in the armoured car (who did indeed desert to the Anti-Treaty Republicans later), or by one of his*

# F Timechart: 1922–49

**1922** *June* Civil War broke out between supporters of the Anglo–Irish Treaty and those against it.
*August* Arthur Griffith died. Michael Collins was assassinated.

**1923** Civil War ended.

**1926** Eamonn de Valera founded Fianna Fail party.

**1932** Fianna Fail won the General Election in the Irish Free State.

**1936** *18 June* Fianna Fail Government outlawed the IRA following a number of civilian murders.
About 200–300 IRA soldiers fought for the Republicans in the Spanish Civil War (1936–39).

**1937** A new constitution of Eire replaced the Irish Free State. It did not recognise the existence of a separate state of Northern Ireland.
*Summer* The IRA blew up customs posts on the border with Northern Ireland to protest against a visit by the King and Queen of Britain.

**1939** Led by a new Chief of Staff, Sean Russell, the IRA carried out a series of bomb attacks in England.
*September* Outbreak of Second World War. Russell and the IRA collaborated with the Germans. Eire remained neutral. The Unionists supported Britain.

**1940** *May* Hermann Goertz, a German agent, parachuted into Ireland to work with the IRA.

**1941** Goertz arrested and interned.

**1945** End of the Second World War.
*July* A Labour government came to power in Britain. As part of the United Kingdom, citizens of Northern Ireland benefited from the new Welfare State – with social services such as free education and the National Health Service.

**1948** Fianna Fail lost the general election in Eire.

**1949** Eire officially became the Republic of Ireland. Britain accepted this, but promised to support the continued existence of Northern Ireland as part of the United Kingdom.

closest colleagues, Emmet Dalton, it was also said that the whole ambush had been engineered by de Valera, who was indeed in the area at the time . . . The truth seems to have been that as the firing died down and the ambush seemed to be over Collins stood up in the road and was hit either directly by a last lone sniper from the ridge above or by a ricochet. Emmet Dalton ran up the road and whispered . . . into the ear of the man he knew to be dying if not already dead from a gaping wound in the back of his head.* (G)

The Civil War ended in defeat for those who opposed the Treaty and partition of Ireland. However, in 1932 de Valera's Anti-Treaty party, Fianna Fail, won the General Election in the Irish Free State and changed its name to Eire. The Roman Catholic Church was given a special importance in the new *constitution* (laws for the country):

*'The State acknowledges that the homage of public worship is due to Almighty God . . . The State recognises the special position of the Holy Catholic Apostolic and Roman Catholic Church as the guardian of Faith professed by the great majority of the citizens.* (H)

De Valera had plans for a Republic of all Ireland. It was not until 1948 that Eire became the Republic of Ireland. The British Government accepted this but has continued to support partition. Protestant Unionists have no wish to be a part of a Catholic United Ireland. Meanwhile, the IRA, which was declared illegal in Southern Ireland in June 1936, has continued the fight for a United Independent Republic of Ireland down to the present day.

## ??????????????

**1** Look at evidence **A–E**.
**a** Why were Michael Collins and Arthur Griffith willing to sign the Peace Treaty?
**b** Why were other Nationalists like Eamon de Valera against it?
**c** Why might supporters of the Treaty have reason to fear the men in **E**?

**2** Look at **G**
**a** Is this primary or secondary evidence?
**b** According to this account, who could have killed Michael Collins?
**c** What other evidence might support the conclusion that Collins was killed by a sniper or a ricochet?
**d** What might Emmet Dalton have whispered into Collins' ear?

**3** What might Protestant Unionists think of **H** and the new constitution?

# 19 The Orange State: A Bloody Beginning

Nationalists living in Northern Ireland supported Sinn Fein in the 1919–21 War of Independence, which led to the partition of Ireland (see pages 32–33). Protestant Unionists reacted by trying to get rid of Sinn Fein in the North. In a speech at an Orange rally near Belfast, the Unionist Edward Carson declared:

*We must proclaim today clearly that, come what will and be the consequences what they may, we in Ulster will tolerate no Sinn Fein – no Sinn Fein methods . . . I hate words without action.* (A)

On 12 July 1920 members of the Belfast Protestant Association attacked Catholic workers at Workman, Clark and Co's shipyard. One of the workers described the attack:

*Men armed with sledge-hammers and other weapons swooped down on Catholic workers in the shipyards and didn't give them a chance for their lives . . . The gates were smashed down with sledges, the vests and shirts of those at work were torn open to see if the men were wearing any Catholic emblems, and then woe betide the man who was. One man was set upon, thrown into the dock, had to swim the Musgrave Channel, and having been pelted with rivets had to swim two or three miles, to emerge in streams of blood and rush to the police office in a nude state.* (B)

In September 1920 the Unionist leader, James Craig, persuaded the British Government to create a special Ulster Constabulary to help the police keep law and order. The British Government was criticised for this in the press:

*The Official proposal to arm 'well-disposed' citizens to assist the authorities in Belfast . . . raised serious questions of the sanity of the Government. It seems to me the most outrageous thing which they have ever done in Ireland . . . A citizen of Belfast who is 'well-disposed' to the British Government is, almost from the nature of the case, an Orangeman, or at any rate a vehement anti-Sinn Feiner. These are the very same people who have been looting Catholic shops and driving thousands of Catholic women and children from their homes.* (C)
London Daily News, 15 September 1920

The Government of Ireland Act partitioned Ireland in 1920. Both Protestants and Catholics were upset about where the boundaries between Northern and Southern Ireland were fixed. Map D shows how the boundaries were drawn. Northern Ireland was made up of the six North-Eastern counties, where Protestants outnumbered Catholics by two to one. This angered the 70 000 Protestants who lived in the three Ulster counties which had been included in Southern Ireland. They wanted to be part of the North.

In several parts of Northern Ireland, like Fermanagh (see E), Catholics outnumbered Protestants, although they were in the minority overall. Catholics did not want partition. Many continued to support the Nationalists in the war for an independent, united Ireland. The Unionists saw this as a threat against their wish to remain part of the United Kingdom of Great Britain, separate from Southern Ireland.

Some non-Unionists were intimidated during the elections for the new Home Rule Parliament of Northern Ireland:

*No sooner has it been discovered that a man is a Sinn Fein election agent for a district than he has disappeared . . . At Martial Hall in Armagh the Sinn Fein director of elections for the district was taken out of his house by the Specials (the*

### D  The partition of Ireland

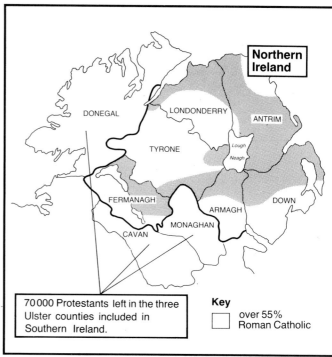

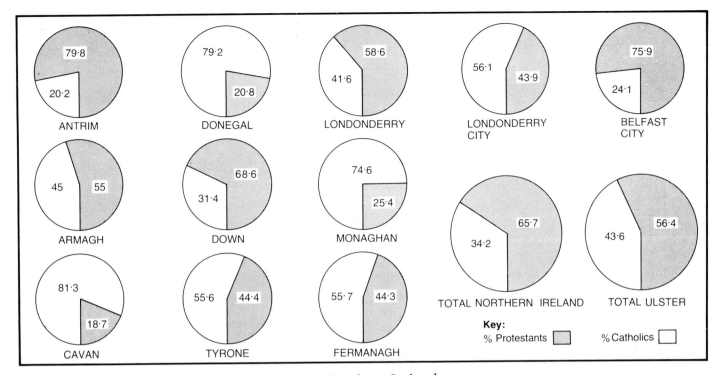

E  Proportions of Catholics and Protestants in Northern Ireland

Special Ulster Constabulary) . . . *and made to go down upon his knees and promise he would take no further part in the elections.* ) **(F)**    *The Manchester Guardian, 21 May 1921*

The Unionists won 40 seats in the new parliament and the Nationalists 12 seats (six of these went to Sinn Fein members). James Craig became Prime Minister of the Unionist Government. On 22 June 1921 King George V travelled to open the new Parliament at Stormont in Belfast.

The failure of peace talks between the British Government and Irish Nationalists led to more Unionist attacks on Catholics in Northern Ireland. As the police and special Ulster Constabulary did not stop the attacks, Catholics in Northern Ireland looked to the IRA for protection:

*After a disinterested investigation, the conclusion one has been forced to is, that the blame for beginning the troubles lies at the door of the Orangemen, and that, for the desperate shooting of Monday and Tuesday, both sides must bear responsibility, with this point to be remembered in favour of the Catholics, that, as they were attacked and as there was no military protection available, the members of the IRA retaliated in kind and quite as effectively . . .* ) **(G)**
*The Manchester Guardian, 27 August 1921*

In June 1921, 40 per cent of the population in Northern Ireland was out of work. Competition for jobs added to the tension between Protestants and Catholics. Over 10 000 Catholics in Belfast were forced to leave their jobs. Over 500 Catholic businesses were wrecked. Between July 1920 and July 1922, 453 people were murdered in Belfast, compared with 106 killings in the rest of Ulster. Of those killed in Belfast 257 were Catholics, 157 were Protestants, two were of unknown religion and 37 were policemen or soldiers.

## ??????????????

**1** How might a Catholic Sinn Fein supporter living in Belfast react to news of the following:
  **a** partition?
  **b** the treatment of Catholic workers at the Workman, Clark & Co shipyard?
  **c** the setting up of the Special Ulster Constabulary?
  **d** the elections for the new Home Rule Parliament of Northern Ireland?
  **e** the visit of the King to open the new Parliament?

**2** Why were both Protestants and Catholics upset about where the boundaries of Northern Ireland were drawn?

**3** How might a Protestant Unionist justify the treatment of Catholics outlined in this chapter?

**4** Look at **C** and **F**.
  **a** What evidence is there of bias in these reports?
  **b** How reliable is the Manchester Guardian as a historical source?
  **c** How could a historian check the facts in these accounts?

# 20 The Unionists Increase Control 1922–45

Fears that Catholics would support a Nationalist rebellion hardened the attitudes of Protestants and the Government.

The police – the Royal Ulster Constabulary – recruited many more Protestants than Catholics. Catholics were supposed to form a third of the force, but in 1922 less than a sixth was Catholic. This was because most Catholics saw the RUC as a tool of the Unionist Government. Extra men were recruited into the RUC from the 'Specials', (A). These were volunteer part-time policemen from the Special Ulster Constabulary. They did not have to meet the normal entrance requirements for the police force, and they were allowed to carry arms. Most of the 'specials' were Protestants, and many were ex-members of the Ulster Volunteer Force. They were badly-disciplined and often beat up Catholic rioters. Most Catholics feared and hated the 'B-Specials' as they were called.

A Special Powers Act passed in April 1922 gave the RUC more power than any other police force in the United Kingdom, (B).

To Catholics this law seemed to be used more against them than against Protestants. They called it an 'Orange' law. Even when they were given a trial, Catholics had reason to believe that judges would be biased:

*By 1970, out of seven judges of the High Court, three were former Unionist MPs at Stormont (The Northern Ireland Parliament); a fourth was the son of a Unionist Minister.*
(C)

The local elections of 1920 brought a threat to the Protestants when Catholics won some control over local

A  The 'Specials' in action against rioters

## B  The terms of the Special Powers Act

1 People suspected of crimes could be arrested and kept in prison without a trial (interned) for as long as the Government wished.
2 Newspapers could be prevented from printing certain reports.
3 Houses could be searched without a warrant.
4 People were less free to go where they liked.
5 The authorities did not have to hold inquests on any dead bodies found in Northern Ireland.
6 People who had anything to do with explosives, firearms, causing fires and blackmail could be punished by whipping (until 1968).

government. Nationalists gained control of 25 out of 80 councils. These included County Councils like Fermanagh and the City Council of Londonderry. How was this possible when the majority of the population in Northern Ireland was Protestant and voted Unionist? The answer was *Proportional Representation* (PR). Under this system the number of politicians elected depended upon the number of votes cast for each party, instead of the number of votes for each candidate. The purpose of PR was to give the Catholic minority some say in the local government of Northern Ireland. This did not suit the Unionists. In 1922 the Unionist Government abolished PR.

A special Commission was set up to draw the boundaries for voting districts in local elections. Catholics refused to take part in the Commission because they preferred PR. To make sure that Unionists did better than Nationalists in local elections the *Gerrymander* was used. D shows how it worked.

In the local elections of 1924, Nationalists won control of only two out of 80 councils. The Unionists now had firm control of Northern Ireland. But how long would it last?

Northern Ireland was the poorest part of the United Kingdom. Though the Unionist Government controlled law and order and local government, the British Government controlled the economy. Britain did not give the Unionist Government enough money to overcome the serious problems of poor housing, poor health and education services and unemployment. The world economic depression of the 1930s hit Northern Ireland

In 1966 the adult population of Derry was 30 376. There were 20 102 Catholics; 10 274 Protestants. Yet there were more Protestant Unionist than Nationalist councillors. Why?

**THE GERRYMANDER**
1  More Protestants than Catholics became boundary commissioners (Catholics refused).
2  They had to draw up the boundaries of the voting districts.
3  They drew boundaries which favoured Protestants.
4  More Protestant councillors were elected.

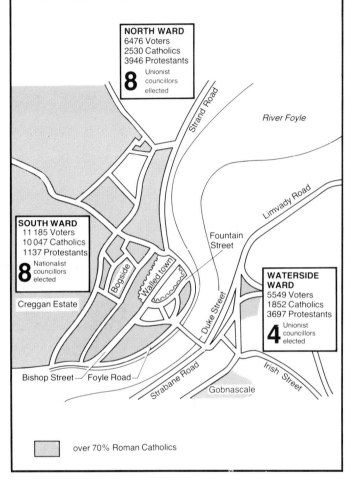

**D  How the Gerrymander worked**

hard (see **E**). Between 1930–39, 25 per cent of the workforce were unemployed.

The Second World War (1939–45) once again put the loyalty of Ulstermen and women to the test. 4500 died fighting for Britain. Thousands lost their homes in German air raids on Belfast in 1941. The British Prime Minister, Winston Churchill (the son of Randolph Churchill, see pages 22–23) said on 20 May 1943:

*But for the loyalty of Northern Ireland and its devotion . . . we should have been faced with slavery and death . . . The bonds of affection between Great Britain and the people of Northern Ireland have been tempered by fire and are now, I firmly believe, unbreakable . . .* (F)

**E  Table of events: 1922–45**

1922  *April*  The Unionist Government formed the RUC and passed the Special Powers Act.
*June*  Civil War broke out between Republicans who accepted the Anglo–Irish Treaty and those against it.
*September*  The Unionist Government abolished proportional representation at local elections. Later the Unionists abolished proportional representation for the Northern Ireland Parliament.

1932  High unemployment and poverty sparked off riots.

1933  The Special Powers Act was made permanent.

1935  Orange Order marches led to riots.

1937  The IRA campaign to re-unite Ireland revived.

1939  The IRA started a bombing campaign in Britain. The Second World War started. 38 000 Ulstermen and women fought for Britain. 4500 lost their lives.

1941  The Belfast Blitz. German air raids killed 898 people and left thousands homeless.

1943  Sir Basil Brooke became Prime Minister of Northern Ireland.

1945  The Second World War ended.

# ??????????????

**1 a** Why was the Royal Ulster Constabulary unable to recruit more Catholics?
**b** Suggest two reasons why entrance standards were not enforced for recruiting members of the Specials.
**c** Why were many Catholics afraid of the 'B-Specials'?
**d** With what justification did the Catholics call the 1922 Special Powers Act an 'Orange' law?

**2** Imagine you are a Catholic in Northern Ireland in 1923. Write a letter to your Unionist MP protesting against *one* of the following: **a** the Special Powers Act; **b** the 'B-Specials'; **c** the abolition of proportional representation.

**3** Look at **D**. How would you redraw the boundaries of Derry to produce a fair number of Catholic Councillors?

# 21 Liberal Unionism, 1945–63

Look at the figures in **A**.

**A**

| Percentage of the workforce unemployed in Great Britain (England, Scotland and Wales) | | Northern Ireland |
|---|---|---|
| **December 1922** | 14.1 | 22.9 |
| **February 1938** | 12.8 | 29.5 |
| **December 1955** | 1.0 | 6.7 |
| **July 1980** | 6.5 | 12.1 |

What do you notice about the level of unemployment in Northern Ireland compared with the rest of the United Kingdom? In the 1930s unemployed Protestants and Catholics sometimes united in protest, as this mill worker remembered:

*There was no work so we decided that we would march to the workhouse on the Lisburn Road and march we did. Many marched in their bare feet . . . the Falls and the Shankhill united.* (**B**)

A survey in 1938 showed that the death rate in Northern Ireland was 25 per cent higher than in the rest of the United Kingdom. The main cause of this was *not* violence but poverty. Poor housing, bad public health, and poor medical services led to illness and disease among Protestants and Catholics alike. Poor diet meant that children of the unemployed in Belfast were on average as much as seven centimetres shorter and four kilograms lighter than children of employed parents in the same city.

After the Second World War (1939–45) the United Kingdom became a Welfare State. As a part of the United Kingdom the people of Northern Ireland could take advantage of social services and benefits which were not available in Southern Ireland. For the first time, many Catholics saw that there were some things to be said in favour of union with Great Britain, as Eamonn McCann commented:

*The development of the Welfare State under the British Labour Government . . . compulsory national insurance, increased family allowance and the Health Service, all helped to shield Catholics from the worse effects of unemployment and poverty. Pressure to emigrate was reduced . . . And since benefits were not available south of the border the tendency to regard achievement of a United Ireland as the only way to make things better began to weaken.*

*The overall effect on the Northern Ireland Catholics of postwar change was a lessening urgency about the border coupled with growing impatience about discrimination.* (**C**)

(*War and an Irish Town*)

**D** The Territorial Army headquarters at Enniskillen after an IRA bombing raid

Although some Catholics were beginning to think that a United Ireland was not the only way to make things better, many Nationalists were still determined to end partition. In 1956 the IRA launched a new campaign 'Operation Harvest' against the Unionist Government of Northern Ireland. **D** shows what the IRA did to the territorial army headquarters at Enniskillen, in January 1957. The campaign ended in 1962. One reason for its failure was that the British secret service, MI5, was used to track down IRA men. Those who escaped to Southern Ireland were captured and imprisoned.

The IRA gave another reason:

*'The decision to end the resistance campaign has been taken in view of the general situation. Foremost among the facts motivating this course of action has been the attitude of the general public whose minds have been deliberately distracted from the supreme issue facing the Irish people – the unity and freedom of Ireland.'* (E)

In 1963 Captain Terence O'Neill (**F**) became Unionist Prime Minister of Northern Ireland. Though a Protestant and a member of the Orange Order his attitude towards the Catholic minority seemed more sympathetic and liberal than the Unionist leaders before him:

*'. . . let us at least be united in working together in a Christian spirit to create better opportunities for our children, whether they come from the Falls Road (a Catholic area) or from Finaghy (a Protestant area) . . . let us shed the burden of traditional grievances and ancient resentments.'* (G)

Terence O'Neill tried to bring Protestants and Catholics together. He believed that better standards of living, better education and more goodwill would solve the Irish question. New industries and better trade would create more jobs. O'Neill believed that Northern Ireland and the Irish Republic should see if they could help each other. In 1965 he invited Sean Lemass, *Taoiseach* (Prime Minister) of the Irish Republic, to Belfast. Afterwards they said of their friendly talks:

*'There may prove to be a further degree of common interest and we have agreed to explore further what specific measures may be possible or desirable by way of practical consultation and co-operation. Our talks – which did not touch upon constitutional or political questions – have been conducted in a most amicable way and we look forward to a further discussion in Dublin.'* (H)

Meanwhile, serious trouble was brewing. Catholics wanted changes in Northern Ireland and now expected O'Neill to make them. On the other hand, many Protestants thought he had gone too far already!

F  Captain Terence O'Neill

# ??????????????

**1 a** According to **A**, which part of the United Kingdom has suffered most from unemployment since 1922?
**b** Why was the death rate in Northern Ireland in the 1930s 25% higher than in the rest of the United Kingdom?

**2** What might an Ulster Catholic say, in 1965, in favour of Union with Great Britain?

**3 a** Why do you think the IRA chose targets like **D** to blow up during 'Operation Harvest'?
**b** Give three reasons why the IRA campaign ended in failure. Which did the IRA think was most important? Which do you think was most important?

**4 a** What did Captain Terence O'Neill do to raise the hopes of Catholics living in Northern Ireland after 1963?
**b** Why might a Protestant living in Ulster be suspicious of what O'Neill was doing?

# 22 Catholic Grievances

Catholics living in Northern Ireland knew there was discrimination against them over employment (see page 17). In 1959, at a time of rising unemployment, the Reverand Ian Paisley and his followers formed 'Ulster Protestant Action' (UPA). Its purpose was:

*'to keep Protestants and loyal workers in employment in times of depression in preference to their fellow Catholic workers.'* (A)

### D  Timechart

| | |
|---|---|
| 1956 | Beginning of IRA campaign 'Operation Harvest'. The Protestant preacher, Rev. Ian Paisley, won publicity for 'saving a fifteen-year-old Catholic girl from being shut up in a nunnery against her will'. |
| 1959 | Paisley was again in the news for throwing a bible at Methodist preacher Lord Soper, who preached in favour of Church unity between Catholics and Protestants. Ulster Protestant Action was formed by Paisley and his supporters, at a time of rising unemployment. |
| 1962 | IRA ended 'Operation Harvest'. |
| 1963 | Sir Basil Brooke, Unionist Prime Minister for 20 years, was replaced by Captain Terence O'Neill. Patricia McCluskey formed the Homeless Citizens League in Dungannon to protest against discrimination against Catholics over Council houses. |
| 1964 | *January* Dr Con and Patricia McCluskey founded the Campaign for Social Justice, to collect and publicise information about injustice in Northern Ireland. The Unionist Government promised reforms and announced an ambitious plan to build new houses and create jobs. During the General Election a Republican flag was displayed at Sinn Fein headquarters in Belfast. This was illegal. It sparked off protests by Protestants, leading to riots. |
| 1965 | A meeting was held between Terence O'Neill and Sean Lemass, Taoiseach of the Irish Republic. This infuriated many Protestants. |

In County Fermanagh over half the population is Catholic. In 1961, an investigation by the *Sunday Times* newspaper found that:

*'The County Council itself employed 370 people: 332 of the posts, including all the top ones, were filled by Protestants. On the County Education Authority the most coveted (wanted) jobs were the ones for school bus drivers, because of the long rests and long holidays. Of about 75 school bus drivers in Fermanagh, all but seven were Protestant.'* (B)

The UPA was helped by the 'unfair' local election system – the Gerrymander (see pages 38–39), and by the fact that:

*'Businessmen – mainly Protestants – had extra votes; many of the Catholic poor had none . . . sub-tenants, lodgers and children over 21 living at home did not (have the vote). About 25 000 adults were thus disenfranchised (did not have the*

E  Housing conditions in the Bogside area of Londonderry

vote) *for local government elections. The great bulk of these were Catholics.* **(C)**

Out of 52 Councillors the Fermanagh County Council had 35 Protestant Unionist Councillors. The Council Chairman in 1961 was Captain John Brooke, son of Lord Brookeborough (see **D**) who had himself been Council Chairman for 15 years.

Source **E** shows Patrick Doherty and his nine-year-old daughter in the backyard of their home in Londonderry's Catholic Bogside area. In 1961, 19.3 per cent of houses in Northern Ireland had no piped water supply; 22.6 per cent had no flush toilets. As well as providing jobs, local councils also provide houses. According to the *Sunday Times*:

*'There are several ways in which Protestant councils have discriminated against Catholics. One has been to put Protestants in better houses than Catholics, but charge the same rents. In Dungannon, for an identical rent, you got 42 square feet of space less on the mainly Catholic Ballymurphy Estate than you got on the exclusively Protestant Cunningham's Lane Estate. Another way has simply been to house more Protestants than Catholics, of 1589 houses built by Fermanagh County Council between the end of the Second World War and 1969, 1021 went to Protestant families.'* **(F)**

Catholics felt frustrated and angry. In 1963 Patricia McClusky took direct action against her local council of Dungannon by forming a Homeless Citizens League. The following year her husband Dr Con McClusky founded the Campaign for Social Justice (see **D**).

The new Unionist Prime Minister, Terence O'Neill, promised reforms and improvements. He promised to get rid of the extra votes for businessmen and universities. In 1965, he promised to build 12 000 new houses a year and find 65 000 new jobs by 1970. By March 1965, 234 businesses had started up in Northern Ireland, 40 per cent of which were British.

Source **G** shows a housing estate in the new city of Craigavan. O'Neill wanted Protestants and Catholics to live together in cities like this. A Catholic family called the Sands moved to an estate like this. But hostile Protestants drove them back to the safety of a Catholic housing estate. Bobby Sands, then a young boy, was to join the IRA and later to die on hunger strike in prison (see pages 60–61).

Terence O'Neill wanted to improve relations with the Republic of Ireland. A trade agreement with the Republic was signed in 1965 and O'Neill thought it a good time to invite Sean Lemass, *Taoiseach* (Prime Minister) of the Irish Republic, to Belfast for talks (see pages 40–41). Ian Paisley and his followers were afraid that O'Neill was moving towards unity between

**G** A publicity photograph showing new housing in Craigavan

Northern Ireland and the Irish Republic. Sean Lemass had taken part in the Easter Rising of 1916, the War of Independence, and the Civil War. He had been sent to prison by both British and Irish Free State Governments. To Ian Paisley he was

*'a Fenian Papist Murderer.'* **(H)**

# ??????????????

**1** What does photograph **E** tell us about living conditions in the Catholic Bogside area of Belfast? How reliable is this kind of evidence?

**2 a** Why did Protestants like Ian Paisley openly encourage discrimination against Catholics over jobs in the 1960s?
**b** What evidence is there that Protestants followed the advice of Ulster Protestant Action (**A** and **B**)?

**3** Use **A–F** to list reasons why the Sands family might feel frustrated and angry in 1965.

**4** Imagine you are a journalist for an English 'popular' newspaper. Use the evidence of this section, and anything else you can find, to write a report about the problems of Catholics living in Northern Ireland. Think about: an eye-catching headline; background information needed by your readers; interesting presentation of your story.

# 23 Protestant Fears

Was Paisley right? Would O'Neill's Liberal Unionism lead to the re-uniting of Northern and Southern Ireland? What would this mean for Protestants?

❛*The Roman Catholic Church is the governing force in Eire today . . . The libraries, newspapers and publishing firms in Eire are almost completely dominated by the Roman Catholic outlook . . . in the radio and film world also Rome's control is complete.*

*In Eire . . . the Roman Catholic Church has claimed the exclusive right to train the nation's children . . . Herein lies the secret of priestly power in Eire . . .* ❜ (A)

❛*Only an Orangeman would suggest that the Catholic hierarchy* (leaders of the Roman Catholic Church) *rules the Republic . . . since the state was established the church has rarely interfered directly with its running, yet the Irish Republic is undeniably governed according to a moral code approved by the Catholic Church. The clergy do not need to interfere directly because they have almost complete control over education of 95 per cent of the population.* ❜ (B)

Many Protestants shared Paisley's fear that in a United Ireland, Catholics would outvote Protestants. Protestants might lose control over the education of their children, freedom from some kinds of censorship (C) and freedom to make personal decisions on moral questions like contraception and abortion. In February 1966 Paisley started a newspaper *The Protestant Telegraph* to warn Protestants of the dangers of getting too friendly with Republicans. This paper attacked the

liberal ideas of Terence O'Neill. In April 1966 Paisley also formed an Ulster Constitution Defence Committee to resist the reforms O'Neill had promised Catholics (see pages 40–41).

**D** shows Republicans in Belfast on 12 April celebrating the 50th anniversary of the Dublin Easter Rising of 1916. Parades like this took place all over Ireland in 1966. Ian Paisley was outraged. He called for the Government to ban all Republican parades in Northern Ireland. The Government decided to let the parades go ahead – but they expected trouble. While these parades took place the Government banned trains from the South and called up the 'B-Specials' (see page 38) for duty.

Paisley was also alarmed when in June the General Assembly of the Protestant Presbyterian Church met in Belfast to discuss, among other things, the question of unity between Protestant and Catholic churches. On 6 June Paisley led a protest march which ended in fights with Catholics and a riot. Terence O'Neill accused Paisley and his followers of behaving like 'Nazi gangsters'. Paisley was arrested and sent to prison for three months. Meanwhile, some of his more violent supporters formed a new Ulster Volunteer Force – named after the UVF of 1912–14 (see page 23). They wrote to local newspapers to warn that:

❛*Known IRA men will be executed mercilessly and without hesitation.* ❜ (E)

On 26 June UVF gunmen shot what they mistook to be three IRA leaders as they left a pub in Malvern Street near the Shankill Road in Belfast. The three men were Catholics who worked at the pub. One of them died. The Government used the Special Powers Act (see page 38) to make the UVF illegal. Three UVF men were arrested and sent to prison. But was this enough? On 12 July 1966 Orange marches again reminded Catholics that Northern Ireland was ruled by Protestants. The Catholics were losing patience with O'Neill and his promises. They wanted action. As Catholic unrest increased, the Protestants grew more alarmed.

Basil Brooke (Viscount Brookeborough) was Unionist Prime Minister of Northern Ireland from 1943–63. In a newspaper interview in 1968 he explained why Protestants continued to fear and discriminate against Catholics:

## C  The Catholic church banned these books in the Irish Republic

From 1930 to 46:

Farrell, James T . . . . . . . . . . . . . . . . . . . . *Studs Lonigan (1936)*
Graves, Robert . . . . . . . . . . . . . . . . . . . . . *I, Claudius (1936)*
Greene, Graham . . . . . . . . . . . . . . . . . . *Brighton Rock (1939)*
Hemmingway, Ernest  *For Whom the Bell Tolls (1941)*
Steinbeck, John . . . . . . . . . . . . *The Grapes of Wrath (1940)*

From 1946 to 66:

Amis, Kingsley . . . . . . . . . . . . . . . . . . . . . *Lucky Jim (1954)*
Heller, Joseph . . . . . . . . . . . . . . . . . . . . . . *Catch 22 (1962)*
Murdoch, Iris . . . . . . . . . . . . . . . . . *A Severed Head (1962)*
Satre, Jean Paul . . . . . . . . . . . . . . . *The Age of Reason (1947)*
Thomas, Dylan . . . . *Adventures in the Skin Trade (1955)*
Updike, John . . . . . . . . . . . . . . . . . . . . . . *Rabbit, Run (1962)*

**D** A Republican parade in Belfast

*'What there is, is a feeling of resentment ... that most Roman Catholics are anti-British and anti-Northern Ireland. This is nothing to do with religion at all. But there is this feeling that here is a man who is out to destroy Northern Ireland if he can possibly do it ... They say why aren't we given more higher positions? But how can you give somebody who is your enemy a higher position in order to allow him to come out and destroy you?'* (F)

# ?????????????????????????????????????

**1** Look at **A** and **B**. (**A** was written around 1937, **B** in the 1970s.)
 **a** Was the writer of **A** for or against the Roman Catholic Church?
 **b** In what ways do the writers of **A** and **B** agree? How do they differ?
 **c** How reliable are **A** and **B** as sources of historical evidence?

**2** Using **A–E**, explain why many Protestants were afraid of a United Ireland. Do you think their fears were justified?

**3** For what reasons might the Catholic Church want to stop people reading the books listed in **C**?

**4** Imagine you are an adviser to Terence O'Neill. There are four plans he could follow to put Protestant minds at rest:
 **a** Ignore Catholic complaints and demands for change.
 **b** Drive the Catholics out of Northern Ireland.
 **c** Show that he did not want reunion between the North and the South – but end discrimination against Catholics.
 **d** Improve living standards and employment for Protestants before helping Catholics.
Which plans would you back? For what reasons? Which would you oppose? Why?

# 24 Civil Rights

Television and newspapers in the early 1960s showed scenes like **A**, in the United States of America. Black people had joined together to demand their Civil Rights – rights to go to the same schools as whites, ride in the same buses, eat in the same restaurants and vote in elections. Their methods were *non-violent*. The US Government was shocked into passing laws in 1964 and 1965 to give black and white equal rights.

This success inspired people in other countries who felt they were treated unfairly. In February 1967 members of the Campaign for Social Justice, and of Republican clubs, as well as students and workers, formed the Northern Ireland Civil Rights Association (NICRA). Anyone could join. They aimed to use peaceful, non-violent means to obtain reforms and changes.

At Caledon, near Dungannon, in October 1967, Civil Rights leaders encouraged homeless Catholic families to squat in newly-built council houses. Was this the same as demanding Civil Rights? Some political groups wanted to use NICRA for their own ends. In March 1968 in Londonderry a local Republican club and the left wing local Labour Party formed the Derry Housing Action Committee, led by Eamonn McCann. They too encouraged homeless Catholics to squat and disrupted local government meetings. Their extreme methods seemed to work, as McCann described:

❛*Mr Wilson was living with his wife and two children in a tiny caravan parked up a mucky lane in the Brandywell district . . . (He) had been told by the Corporation Housing Department that he had 'no chance' of a house . . . On 22 June (1968) . . . about ten of us pushed the Wilson's caravan on to Lecky Road and parked it broadside in the middle of the road, stopping all traffic. We distributed leaflets in the surrounding streets calling for support. We then phoned the police, the mayor and the newspapers, inviting each to come and see . . . Before the week was out the Wilsons had been guaranteed a house and ten of us had been summonsed to appear in court for breaking the Road Traffic Act (of) 1951. It was a perfect ending.*❜ **(B)**

McCann was not afraid of violence. By July 1968

❛*Our conscious, if unspoken strategy was to provoke the police into over-reaction and thus spark off mass reaction against the authorities.*❜ **(C)**

This idea had not come from NICRA or the Black Civil Rights Movement. So where had it come from? Look at photograph **D**. It shows a street battle between protesters and police in Paris, in May 1968 (notice the dates of **B** and **C**). All over France at this time there were violent demonstrations by students and workers against the Government. Television news also showed violent clashes between students and police in West Germany. The leaders of these violent protests wanted revolution.

In August 1968 the first Civil Rights March in Northern Ireland took place. About 2500 people marched from Coalisland to Dungannon to protest against discrimination in housing (see **E**). There was widespread coverage of the march in newspapers and on television. It showed that despite anger and frustration about discrimination it was possible for peaceful methods to draw the world's attention to injustices in Northern Ireland.

Who were the supporters of the Civil Rights Association? Protestant Unionists were suspicious. A special investigation was ordered by the British Government in 1969. It found that:

❛*The membership . . . was politically varied in range and undoubtedly included persons of known extreme Republican*

**A**   An American Civil Rights protest in 1964

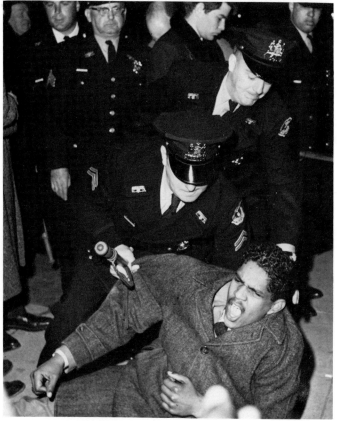

**D** Barricades in the streets of Paris, 1968

*views and activities as well as members of the Northern Ireland and Liberal Parties. In addition, the membership is mostly Roman Catholic in religion . . . it is and always has been a basic rule of the association to place no bar on people from political groups . . . There is no doubt that the IRA has taken a close interest in the Civil Rights Association from its beginning.* (F)

(Cameron Report)

Did this mean that the Civil Rights Association was a 'cover' for the Irish Republican Army?

*The Civil Rights Association maintained that it was non-sectarian (not biased) and concerned only with obtaining reforms and changes in the law, which it sought always by peaceful and non-violent means. It is undoubtedly the case that it has been the policy of the Association to refuse to permit the display of provocative symbols and banners, in particular of the Republican Tricolour, at any demonstration that it has organised or authorised . . .* (G)

(Cameron Report)

The Derry Housing Action Committee invited the Civil Rights Association to hold a march in London-derry. A Committee was set up, representing different political groups, to plan a march for 5 October. However, according to Eamonn McCann:

*By mid-September Eamonn McLough and I had taken effective control . . . None of the placards (prepared for the march) demanded 'civil rights'. We were anxious to assert socialist ideas, whether or not the CRA (Civil Rights Association) approved. We used slogans such as 'Class War not Creed War', 'Orange and Green Tories out', 'Working-Class Unite and Fight' . . .
The CRA was a liberal body not interested in revolutionary politics. But then we were paying little attention to them . . .*
(H)

## E  Timechart

**1967**  *February*  The Northern Ireland Civil Rights Organisation was formed.
*October*  Civil Rights leaders encouraged homeless Catholics in Caledon, near Dungannon, to squat in newly built council houses.

**1968**  *February*  Violent student protests in West Germany.
*March*  Derry Housing Action Committee formed.
*May*  Riots and street fighting in France between police and protesters (see **C**).
*June*  Eviction of Catholic squatters from council houses in Caledon. One of these houses was allocated to a 19-year-old single Protestant girl who was secretary to a Unionist politician. Austin Currie, a Nationalist MP in the Northern Ireland Parliament (Stormont) occupied the house to publicise this discrimination. He was evicted on 20 June.
*24 August*  2500 people marched in first Northern Ireland Civil Rights March from Coalisland to Dungannon.

# ??????????????

**1 a** What methods did the Northern Ireland Civil Rights Association have in common with the Black Civil Rights Movement in the USA?
**b** How did these methods differ from those of the Derry Housing Action Committee and protesters in Paris and Germany?

**2** Look at **F** and **G**. What evidence can you find in the report to suggest that:
**a** Protestant Unionists had reason to be suspicious of the Civil Rights Association?
**b** Unionists were unfair to believe that the Northern Ireland Civil Rights Association was a 'cover' for the IRA?

**3** Imagine you are a Civil Rights supporter in Northern Ireland, in 1967. Draw up a plan of action setting out your aims and how to achieve them.

**4** Put the following into order and suggest the links between them: riots in France and Germany; the formation of the Northern Ireland Civil Rights Association; the Black Civil Rights Movement in the USA; the invitation from Derry Housing Action Committee to hold a Civil Rights march in Londonderry.

# 25 The Unionist Backlash

**B** A Civil Rights demonstration in Londonderry

A Civil Rights March took place in Derry on 5 October 1968. Most of the marchers were Catholics. The route of the march was planned to pass through the centre of the walled city of Londonderry known as the Diamond. The Protestant Unionists were furious about this — no Catholic march had been allowed into the Diamond for almost 20 years. The Protestant Apprentice Boys of Londonderry announced that they would parade over the same route on the same day.

Mr William Craig, the Unionist Minister of Home Affairs, banned both marches. Despite this ban the Civil Rights March took place. One of the marchers was Eamonn McCann, who helped form the Derry Housing Action Committee (see pages 46–47) and was an active campaigner against the ill-treatment of Catholics. He described what happened:

*Our route was blocked by a cordon of police and tenders drawn up across the road about 300 yards from the starting point. We marched into the police cordon but failed to force a way through. Gerry Fitt's (a Civil Rights leader and MP) head was bloodied by the first blow of the day. We noticed that another police cordon had marched in from the rear and cut us off from behind . . .*

*The two police cordons moved simultaneously on the crowd. Men, women and children were clubbed to the ground. People were fleeing down the street from the front cordon and up the street from the rear cordon, crashing into one another, stumbling over one another, huddling in doorways, some screaming. District Inspector Ross McGimpsie, chief of the local police (now promoted) moved in behind his men and laid about him with gusto. The Bogside was filled with journalists . . . Derry was big news. The Prime Minister, Captain Terence O'Neill made a liberal speech appealing for moderation and restraint. Mr Craig praised the police for their tactful handling of the affair.* (A)

All over Ireland and Great Britain television viewers saw the march and the violence that resulted (B). The Royal Ulster Constabulary's violent methods shocked and angered many people. The Northern Ireland Civil Rights Association gained more support. But its leaders were worried that the violence would give people the wrong impression. To make it clear what they wanted:

*. . . Following the march of 5 October 1968 . . . a definite programme calling for specific reforms was adopted and publicised. These may be summarised thus —*

*1 The vote for everybody as in the rest of the United Kingdom.
2 The redrawing of electoral boundaries by an independent commission to ensure fair representation.
3 Laws against discrimination in employment at local government level.
4 A compulsory points system for housing which would ensure fair allocation.
5 The repeal of the Special Powers Act (see page 38).
6 The disbanding of the Ulster Special Constabulary (B-Specials) . . .* (C)

In January 1969 students from Queen's University Belfast, calling themselves 'People's Democracy', led a Civil Rights March from Belfast to Londonderry. The leaders of the Civil Rights Association were against the march because it went through areas which were strongly Protestant. The march was ambushed at Burntollet Bridge (D). Bernadette Devlin was one of the students:

*And then we came to Burntollet Bridge, and from lanes at each side of the road a curtain of bricks and boulders and bottles brought the march to a halt. From the lanes burst hordes of screaming people wielding planks of wood, bottles, lathes, iron crow bars, cudgels studded with nails, and they waded into the march beating hell out of everybody . . . I saw a young fellow getting a thrashing from four or five Paisleyites, with a policeman looking on . . . .* (E)

When the marchers arrived in Londonderry rioting broke out in the city. **F** and **G** were written by Eamonn McCann in 1973:

*Of the 80 who had set out fewer than 30 arrived in Derry uninjured. But they had gathered hundreds of supporters behind them on the way and were met in Guildhall Square by angry thousands who were in no mood for talk of truce. Emotion swelled as bloodstained marchers mounted a platform and described their experiences. Rioting broke out and continued for some hours . . .* (F)

*The area (a Catholic Area of Derry) was peaceful and deserted at 2 am when a mob of policemen came from the city centre through Butcher Gate and surged down Fahan Street into St Columb Wells and Lecky Road, shouting and singing:
'Hey, hey we're the monkees,
And we're going to monkey around
Till we see your blood flowing
All along the ground.'
They broke in windows with their batons, kicked doors and shouted to the people to 'come out and fight, you Fenian bastards'. Anyone who did come to his or her door was grabbed and beaten up.* (G)

An official report for the British Government said:

*. . . Our investigations have led us to the unhesitating conclusion that on the night of 4/5 January a number of policemen were guilty of misconduct which involved assault and battery, malicious damage to property in the streets in the mostly Catholic Bogside area . . . and the use of provocative sectarian and political slogans.* (H) (Cameron Report)

# ??????????????

**1** Write captions for pictures **B** and **D** for both a Protestant and a Catholic newspaper.

**2** Look at evidence **A–C**
  **a** Why was the Civil Rights March banned?
  **b** Do you consider McCann to be a biased witness in **C**?
  **c** Which details of McCann's story (**A**) are supported by the evidence in **B**? Which are not?

**3** Why did the events of October 1968 increase support for the Civil Rights Association?

**4 a** Was Mr Craig right to 'praise the police for their tactful handling of the affair' (**A**)?
  **b** What does the evidence on these pages suggest about the actions of the police?
  **c** Which do you think is the most convincing evidence of police violence?
Give reasons for your answers.

**5** Imagine you are a television News reporter. Describe the problems you face in making an accurate and unbiased film about the events shown in sources **A–H**.

D The battle at Burntollet Bridge

# 26 Troops In!

In 1969 Terence O'Neill's Protestant Unionist Government finally lost control of events in Northern Ireland (see A). Unable to trust the police to protect them, Catholics living in the Bogside area of Derry built barricades across the roads to defend themselves. In March and April bombs damaged electricity supply lines and water works. This was believed to be the work of the IRA, but was really done by the UVF.

By this time Terence O'Neill had lost the support of his Unionist Party. On 28 April he resigned, and his cousin, Major Chichester-Clark, became the new Unionist Prime Minister. In a newspaper interview in May, O'Neill was reported to have said:

*'It's frightfully hard to explain to Protestants that if you give Roman Catholics a good job and a good house they will live like Protestants, because they will see neighbours with cars and television sets . . . They will refuse to have 18 children, but if a Roman Catholic is jobless and lives in the most ghastly hovel, he will rear 18 children on National Assistance . . . If you treat Roman Catholics with due consideration and kindness, they will live like Protestants in spite of the authoritative nature of their church . . .'* (B)

Protestant Orange marches were planned for 12 July. These Orange marches sparked off serious riots in several parts of Northern Ireland. More trouble was expected during the marches in August. The most important parade was the Apprentice Boys' parade on 12 August, in Derry. It was held to commemorate the seige of Derry and celebrate Protestant victories. Every year it reminded Catholics of the power of the Protestants. Many people wanted the parade to be stopped, but Major Chichester-Clark and the Stormont Government refused to ban it.

## A  Timechart: 1969

*5 January* Following attacks by police and Protestant Unionists, Catholics in the Bogside area of Londonderry built barricades to defend themselves.

*24 February* Northern Ireland General Election. Terence O'Neill lost support for his programme of reforms.

*March/April* Bombs caused millions of pounds worth of damage to electricity supply lines and water works. Thought at the time to be the work of the IRA, they were in fact planted by the UVF. O'Neill decided to go ahead with his 'one man, one vote' reform.

*17 April* Bernadette Devlin, a leader of People's Democracy, was elected MP for mid-Ulster (a seat in the British Parliament) at the age of 21. She had the help of the IRA, who did not put up a candidate against her.

*28 April* Terence O'Neill resigned. He was replaced by Major Chichester-Clark.

*12–13 July* Failure to ban the Orange marches resulted in serious riots in several parts of Northern Ireland.

*12 August* The Battle of the Bogside broke out, following the Apprentice Boys March in Londonderry. Bernadette Devlin was given a six month prison sentence for her part in the fighting. She appealed against her sentence.

*13 August* Jack Lynch, Prime Minister of the Irish Republic, made a strong speech on television criticising the Northern Ireland Government.

*14 August* The British Army was sent onto the streets of Northern Ireland to restore law and order.

C  'The Battle of the Bogside', August 1969

Thousands of Orangemen came to Derry from all over Northern Ireland for the march. The route went through the centre of the city, and then around the Catholic Bogside area. As the parade came near the Bogside the Orangemen were stoned. Compare photograph **C** with Eamonn McCann's description:

*'As the volume of stone-throwing increased a mixed force of RUC and supporters of the Apprentice Boys made a charge into the area, which was the signal for the real hostilities to begin. The battle lasted for about 48 hours. Barricades went up all around the area, open-air petrol-bomb factories were established, dumpers hijacked from a building site were used to carry stones to the front. Teenagers went on to the roof of the block of High Flats and began lobbing petrol bombs at the police below.'* (D)

Newspapers and television were eager for good pictures of what was called 'The Battle of the Bogside'. **E** was taken on 13 August. Is it a genuine action picture or a cheap publicity stunt?

Alarmed by what was happening, Jack Lynch, Taoiseach of the Irish Republic, made a strong speech on television:

*'It is evident that the Stormont Government (the Government of Northern Ireland) is no longer in control of the situation. Indeed the present situation is the inevitable outcome of the policies pursued for decades by successive Stormont Governments. It is clear that the Irish Government can no longer stand by and see innocent injured and perhaps worse.'* (F)

The violence spread. What was it like to be caught in the middle of it? This is how Alan the hero of *Under Goliath* (see page 13) described it:

*'We were really bashed to bits. People were screaming and sobbing and shouting with wild, mad shouts . . . And then I could hardly believe my eyes. Streaks of fire came through the air, golden blobs trailing across the black sky like rockets. Over our heads they went and smashed on the street. Whoosh! and pools of fire splashed on the road. Everywhere you looked you could see them: the milk bottles flaming across the darkness and exploding in rivers of flame.'* (G)

Local dairies in Londonderry alone reported the loss of 43 000 milk bottles during the course of one week!

On 14 August 1969 the British Army was sent onto the streets of Londonderry and Belfast to help the police to restore law and order:

*'Powdered with fine ash, exhausted by bloodshed, and brought under order by the arrival of more British troops, the grim city of Belfast settled down late tonight to what looked like being its first night's sleep since Wednesday . . .*

**E** A masked boy, armed with a home made petrol bomb. Is this photograph a fake?

*It (the Army) was greeted with profound relief on the Catholic side, where community leaders had been attempting all day to communicate their plight after last night's widespread house-burning and shooting by Protestant extremists and police. But the troops were met with a cold and hostile reaction from many on the Protestant side . . .'* (H)

*The Observer, 17 August 1969*

## ????????????????

**1 a** Why was trouble expected in Londonderry on 12 August 1969?
**b** Why do you think the Northern Ireland Government refused to ban the Orange marches of July and August 1969?
**c** What in **D** suggests that the RUC and supporters of the Apprentice Boys were on the same side?
**d** Which details of McCann's description (**D**) are supported by photographs **C** and **E**?

**2** Do you think photograph **E** is real or 'set-up'? Why? Why might photographers want to stage a picture like this?

**3** Look at **H**. How were the British troops welcomed by the people of Londonderry and Belfast? How would you account for the friendly reaction of the Catholics and the hostility of Protestants in August 1969?

# 27 An Army of Occupation?

Look at **A** and **B**. What is it like living with the sound of soldiers marching, and army lorries and armoured trucks thundering through the streets? What is it like to be stopped and searched, or have roads blocked off with barbed wire?

At first the Catholics seemed to welcome the British Army, as Eamonn McCann observed:

**A** An armoured patrol car in the streets of Belfast

**B** Army roadblocks set-up after the Londonderry riots, August 1969

*'Immediately after the fighting, relations between the army and most of the people of the area were very good. At Butcher Gate, William Street and other army positions at the edge of the Bogside women squabbled about whose turn it was to take the soldiers their tea . . .'* (C)

**D Timechart: August 1969 – May 1970**

1969　*14 August* The British Army was sent on to the streets of Northern Ireland to help the police to restore law and order.
*19 August* The British Government made the Downing Street Declaration. This supported the continued existence of the Northern Ireland Government but insisted on reforms.
*27 August* James Callaghan, British Home Secretary, visited Northern Ireland, and was well received by Catholics.
*12 September* The Cameron Report was published. This criticised the attitudes and policies of the Unionist Government and upset the Protestant community.
*10 October* The Hunt Report was published. This criticised the RUC for bias and recommended changes. These changes included the disbanding of the B-Specials. They were replaced in 1970 by the Ulster Defence Regiment – part time soldiers under the control of the British Army. Violence broke out as Protestants rioted in the Shankill Road, Belfast. The Army got involved and killed two Protestants.
*November* The IRA split. By 1970 there were two main groups: the Official IRA and the Provisional IRA.

1970　*1–2 April* Riots after Orange Marches. The Army's use of CS gas against Catholic riots helped the Provisional IRA recruit members.
Petrol bomb attacks on Protestant businesses. Army raids in search of weapons in Catholic homes.
*May* Charles Haughey and Neil Blaney were dismissed from the Fianna Fail Government in the Irish Republic, charged with smuggling guns to the IRA. Later acquitted (cleared).

Protestants were not so friendly. The British Labour Government had ordered the British Army to help the Unionist Government to restore law and order. On 19 August the British Government made it clear that changes would have to be made (see **D**):

❛in all laws and decisions of the Government every citizen of Northern Ireland is entitled to the same equality of treatment and freedom from discrimination as in the rest of the United Kingdom, no matter what political views or religion.❜ (**E**)

The British Home Secretary, James Callaghan, visited Northern Ireland and promised justice. Special investigations called the Cameron and the Hunt Commissions were set up to find out the causes of the recent violence. In September the Cameron report blamed the troubles on discrimination and police bias against Catholics. On 10 October the Hunt report recommended that the Royal Ulster Constabulary should be disarmed and a new police authority set up with Catholics in it; and that the B-Specials should be disbanded and replaced by the Ulster Defence Regiment.

The Hunt report came out on a Friday evening – but this was a great mistake. Friday evening is 'boozing night'. Drink helped to fuel the fury of the Protestants:

❛The Protestants rose in their anger to demonstrate against the vile things Hunt had said about their wonderful police. They came in their thousands down the Shankill Road, appearing like animals, as if by magic. They then marched to burn the Catholics out of the nearby flats. And as they came down the street, they were halted by a cordon of exactly the police they were marching to defend.❜ (**F**)

**F** was written by Sir Arthur Young, the new Police Chief. The army acted firmly to stop the violence. This impressed the Catholics, as Eamonn McCann commented:

❛The army moved in and battered its way up the Shankill with bloodthirsty enthusiasm. In the shooting two Protestants were killed and a dozen wounded. Many others were beaten or kicked unconscious. Who in the Bogside could doubt that at last law and order were being administered impartially?❜ (**G**)

After the Hunt report some reforms were introduced. For example, on 31 March 1970 the Unionist Government disbanded the B-Specials and in June made changes in the Royal Ulster Constabulary. The government also spent two million pounds on creating new jobs and took steps to end discrimination over local government jobs and council houses. Other reforms were promised, but these changes were too slow to take effect. From the early 1970s Catholic attitudes began to change. Catholics were still suspicious of the Unionist Government, as McCann pointed out:

❛None of it, however, made any difference to the clumps of unemployed teenagers who stood, fists dug deep into their pockets, around William Street in the evenings. Briefly folk-heroes in the heady days of August, praised and patronised by local leaders for their expertise with the stone and the petrol bomb . . . For them at least nothing had changed. 'We'll get nothing out of it. The Orangemen are still in power.'❜ (**H**)

Meanwhile, the IRA had split into two groups. The 'Official' IRA and the 'Provisional' IRA. The 'Officials' were based in Southern Ireland. They wanted to continue the struggle to re-unite Ireland by peaceful methods. The 'Provos', based in Northern Ireland, believed that only force could bring about an end to the British occupation of their country.

During the first six months of 1970 the Provisional IRA recruited new members and collected arms. The British Army knew this. They advised the Unionist Government to ban the Orange Marches due to take place on 1 April. This advice was ignored. Serious rioting broke out in the Ballymurphy estate in West Belfast:

❛When a second night's rioting began in Ballymurphy on the evening of 2 April, 600 troops supported by five Saracen armoured cars moved into the estate. As a show of force it was counter-productive. The Catholic mob showered the troops with stones and bottles. 'I'm not having my men stoned like that,' a senior officer said. The order to use CS gas was given.

The smoke rolled in clouds down the streets and gulleys of the estate, choking rioters and peaceful citizens in their homes alike. The army never grasped that a weapon like CS gas produces a common reaction among its victims: it creates solidarity (a feeling of togetherness) where there was none before. One knowledgeable local thought afterwards that those Ballymurphy riots gave the first great boost to the Provisional IRA recruiting campaign.❜ (**J**)

(*The Sunday Times*)

---

# ??????????????

**1 a** Why did Catholics welcome the British Army at first (**C**, **E**, **G**)?
**b** Why did their attitude change after the early 1970s (**H**)?

**2 a** Why did Protestants react so violently to the Hunt report (**F**)?
**b** Do you think the report was justified? Why?

**3 a** What is the difference between the 'Official' IRA and the 'Provisional' IRA?
**b** Why did the Ballymurphy riots give a 'boost' to the recruiting campaign of the Provisional IRA?

53

# 28 Internment, 1971

*‹ For God's sake bring me a large Scotch. What a bloody awful country. › (A)*

This is what the new Conservative British Home Secretary, Reginald Maudling, was reported to have said as his plane left Northern Ireland in July 1970. He had just been on a visit to find out for himself the cause of the riots and bombings.

By now there were frequent shootings and gun battles between the Provisional IRA and the Ulster Volunteer Force (see **B**). The British Army decided to 'get tough'. On 3 July troops entered the Catholic Lower Falls area of Belfast to search for weapons and ammunition belonging to the Provisional IRA. They took over the whole area and imposed a curfew on the people living there. During the house to house search for arms the soldiers smashed-in doors and broke up furniture, leaving a trail of destruction behind them. At the end of all this they had discovered 30 rifles, 24 shot-guns and 52 pistols – not many, considering that there were 100 000 licensed guns in Northern Ireland.

The action of the British troops upset and alienated the people of the Lower Falls area. Catholics in Belfast began to see the army as another weapon that the Unionist Government would use against them.

The violence got worse. In February 1971 the Provisional IRA shot a soldier – Gunner Curtis. He was the first British soldier to be killed in Northern Ireland since the troops were sent onto the streets in August 1969. The Unionists decided that they needed a stronger leader. In March Brian Faulkner replaced Chichester-

**C** Women bang dustbin lids as a warning signal

**B Table of Events June 1970 – December 1971**

1970 *June* British General Election returned the Conservatives to power. Nothing was done to prevent the Orange Parades.
*27 June* Bernadette Devlin, MP for Mid-Ulster, lost her appeal against her prison sentence for her part in the Battle of the Bogside (Aug 1969). A fierce gun battle took place between the Provisional IRA and the Ulster Volunteer Force in the Short Strand in Belfast.
*30 June* Reginald Maudling's first visit to Northern Ireland as British Home Secretary.
*3 July* Rioting and a very serious clash between Catholics and the Army in the Falls area of Belfast. CS gas was used.
*August* The Social Democratic and Labour Party was formed. The leaders included Gerry Fitt, John Hume and Paddy Devlin.

1971 *New Year* Outburst of 'out of season' violence. The Army and Provisional IRA co-operated to control mobs in the Catholic areas.
*February* First British soldier killed since troops first intervened in 1969. Army searches of Catholic areas provoked further violence. 3 Scottish soldiers were murdered on the outskirts of Belfast.
*20 March* Major Chichester-Clark resigned and was replaced by Brian Faulkner as Unionist Prime Minister.
*June* Brian Faulkner introduced a 'get tough' policy know as the 'June Initiative'.
*9 August* Internment was introduced. The Ulster Defence Association (a central council for loyalist Parliamentary groups) (UDA) was formed.
*November* Paisley's Democratic and Unionist Party was formed.
Compton Report on the alleged ill-treatment of internees was published.
By December the total number of people interned was 1576.

**G** Sinn Fein anti-internment protesters in London

Clark as Prime Minister of Northern Ireland. He had been Minister of Home Affairs from 1959–65. Faulkner believed that internment had defeated the IRA's campaign 'Operation Harvest' at that time (see pages 40–41). He decided to use it again.

9 August 1971, 4.30 am. The people of Northern Ireland awoke to the warning signal of women banging dustbin lids on the pavements, (**C**). Since then, at the same time every year, women in the Catholic districts repeat this to remind everyone of what happened. On that day, the army raided their homes and took away 342 men who had been 'listed' (named as suspects) by the RUC Special Branch. Only two of these men were Protestants. 226 of them were interned. Most were sent to Long Kesh internment camp and shut up in special 'high-security' prison cells, known as 'H-blocks'. Many of those interned complained of ill-treatment:

❛*During all this time the hood was still over my head . . . I was made to stand with my feet wide apart and my hands pressed against a wall. During all this time I could hear a low droning noise, which sounded to me like an electric saw or something of that nature . . . My brain seemed ready to burst . . . They struck me several times on the hands, ribs, kidneys and my knee-caps were kicked. My hood-covered head was banged against the wall . . .*❜ (**D**)

When the British Government investigated these complaints it found that:

❛*Where we have concluded that physical ill-treatment took place, we are not making a finding of brutality on the part of those who handled these complainants. We consider that brutality is an inhuman or savage form of cruelty, and that cruelty implies a disposition to inflict suffering, coupled with indifference to or pleasure in the victims' pain. We do not think it happened here.*❜ (**E**)

Many of those who were 'physically ill-treated' claimed to be prisoners of war. It was said that the British Government had broken Article 17 of an international agreement known as The Geneva Convention of 1948.

❛*No physical or mental torture, nor any other form of coercion, may be inflicted upon prisoners of war to secure from them information of any kind whatever. Prisoners who refuse to answer may not be threatened, insulted or exposed to any unpleasant or disadvantageous treatment of any kind.*❜ (**F**)

Before internment began on 9 August there had been 30 violent deaths in 1971. Its introduction provoked a wave of shootings and explosions which killed a further 143 people. However, by the end of the year the violence had begun to die down, thanks to discoveries of arms and ammunition, and many more arrests. Meanwhile the government had created 7000 new jobs and built 14 662 new houses. Unionist Prime Minister Brian Faulkner believed things were getting better. However, internment had increased the bitterness between the Catholic and Protestant communities. Catholic support for the IRA soared, and their attitude towards the British Government and the army hardened.

Now look at **G**. It was taken in London in August 1971. This was Sinn Fein's answer to Reginald Maulding.

## ??????????????

**1** Fill in the chart below, using a tick for a Protestant's reaction and a cross for a Catholic's reaction

|  | very fair | fair | acceptable | unfair | criminal behaviour |
|---|---|---|---|---|---|
| Maudling's remark |  |  |  |  |  |
| Army behaviour |  |  |  |  |  |
| Killing of Curtis |  |  |  |  |  |
| Internment policy |  |  |  |  |  |
| Arrest of internees |  |  |  |  |  |
| Treatment of internees |  |  |  |  |  |
| Sinn Fein posters |  |  |  |  |  |

**2 a** Why did the British army go into the Lower Falls area of Belfast on 3 July 1970?
  **b** What were the results of their action?

**3 a** What do the posters in **G** tell you about Sinn Fein's attitude towards the British army and Reginald Maudling?
  **b** Why do you think Sinn Fein came to London to make this protest?

# 29 Bloody Sunday!

**A** The Londonderry Civil Rights march on 'Bloody Sunday'

A shows a Civil Rights March in the city of Derry on Sunday 30 January 1972. The marchers intended to go to the Guildhall, through the Catholic Bogside area. Eye-witnesses describe what happened:

❝*It's unfortunate but when we got up there past William Street, here, where we're standing, and up towards Rossville Flats we came under fire. We came under fire from the bottom of the Flats . . . we were also petrol-bombed, and some acid, in fact, was poured on us from the top of the Flats. When we're fired at, we must protect ourselves.*❞ **(B)**

(The Commander of the 1st Battalion of the Parachute Regiment)

❝*It was a massacre. I saw no one shooting at troops. If anybody had been, I would have seen it. I saw only the Army shooting. The British Army should hang its head in shame after today's disgusting violence. They shot indiscriminately (without choosing targets) and everywhere' around them without any provocation. I was administering the last rites to a boy about 15 who had been shot by soldiers in Rossville Street . . .*❞ **(C)**

(Father Bradley, a Catholic Priest)

❝*I do not think, from what I saw, that the IRA opened up first, other than one shot which was fired in William Street. Even if they did, I do not think it would have justified the return of fire into crowds of people in that packed square. I saw three people hit, but I honestly and truly could not see any guns. Nor did I hear any nail bombs or petrol bombs being thrown. I have heard many of these and I know the noise they make.*❞ **(D)**

(A reporter for The Guardian)

❝*I was one of more than a 1000 people lying flat on their faces as the shooting continued. Pinned to the ground, it was impossible to tell who fired the first shots . . .*❞ **(E)**

(A reporter for The Daily Telegraph)

After 'Bloody Sunday', as it became known, a special investigation (the Widgery Report) was ordered by the British Government. The report said:

❝*There was no general breakdown in Army discipline . . . soldiers who identified armed gunmen fired upon them in accordance with the standing orders in the Yellow Card. Each soldier was his own judge of whether he had identified a gunman . . . At one end of the scale, some soldiers showed a high degree of responsibility, at the other . . . firing bordered on the reckless.*❞ **(F)**

13 people were killed. At the inquest, the Londonderry City Coroner had this to say:

❝*It strikes me that the army ran amok that day and they shot without thinking of what they were doing. They were shooting innocent people. These people may have been taking part in a parade that was banned – but I don't think that justifies the firing of live rounds indiscriminately. I say it without reservation – it was sheer unadulterated murder.* **'** (G)

## H  The facts

> *1* On Sunday 30 January 1972 there was a Civil Rights March in the City of Derry to protest against internment (see pages 54–55). After introducing internment the Unionist Government had banned all marches. This march was therefore 'illegal'.
> *2* Rather than risk a riot by attempting to stop it the army decided that the march should be: *'dealt with in as low a key as possible for as long as possible.'*
> *3* 26 barriers were put up to prevent the march from going to the Guildhall and to contain it within the Bogside. The Army Commander ordered that: *'An arrest force is to be held centrally behind the checkpoints and launched in a scoop-up operation to arrest as many hooligans and rioters as possible.'*
> *4* The soldiers given the job of the 'scoop-up operation' were from the First Battalion of the Parachute Regiment ('No. 1 Paras') – specialists in fierce attacks on enemy targets, not crowd control.
> *5* The march went peacefully until crowds gathered at the army barriers to protest against the re-routing of the march. Stones were thrown and insults shouted at the soldiers behind the barriers. Just before 4 pm 'No. 1 Paras' began its 'scoop-up operation'.

Bloody Sunday sparked off more trouble (see **J**). The British Government feared a complete breakdown of law and order. In March 1972, Mr Heath, the Conservative Prime Minister, decided that Britain had no alternative but to take over direct control of the Government of Northern Ireland until a solution to the troubles could be found (see **K**).

**J**  Soldiers use CS gas to disperse rioters in Derry

## K  Table of Events 1972

| | |
|---|---|
| 30 January | Bloody Sunday. The British army shot dead 13 unarmed civilians during a Civil Rights March in Derry. On the day of their funeral angry crowds burned down the British Embassy in Dublin (capital of the Irish Republic), and Bernadette Devlin attacked and punched Reginald Maudling (British Home Secretary) in the face while in the House of Commons. |
| February | Ex-Home Affairs Minister of the Unionist Government, William Craig, formed a new Loyalist movement called the Ulster Vanguard. This brought together a number of Loyalist, Orange and Unionist groups who wanted an end to reforms and the extermination of the IRA. They held rallies in February and March. |
| March | The Northern Ireland Government at Stormont was suspended. Direct Rule from the British Parliament at Westminster, London, was re-introduced. |

# ???????????????

**1** Look at evidence **A–H**
  **a** What was the purpose of the Civil Rights March in Derry on 30 January 1972?
  **b** How did the army plan to deal with the march?
  **c** Why were the marchers prevented from going to the Guildhall? How?
  **d** What reason did the Commander of No 1 Paras give for opening fire on civilians (**B**)?
  **e** Does the evidence support the Coroner's conclusion (**G**) that the army were guilty of 'murder'?
Give reasons for your answers.

**2 a** What decision did British Prime Minister Edward Heath make in March 1972?
  **b** Why did he make this decision?

**3** Imagine you were either a member of No 1 Para or a rioter. Say why you went to the march in Derry on 30 January 1972. Write an account of what you thought, felt, saw, heard and did:
**a** one minute before; **b** at the time; **c** one minute after the scenes in **A** and **J**.

# 30 Power Sharing

1972. In working-class areas of Northern Ireland barricades across the streets keep Catholic and Protestant homes apart. In the story *Across the Barricades* by Joan Lingard Kevin is a Catholic, Sadie a Protestant. They live in Belfast. When they start going out together there is trouble. Both families are upset and try to stop them. Neighbours start to talk. One night Kevin is badly beaten up. His sister, Brede, goes to tell Sadie:

❝ *Brede advanced into the warren of Protestant streets with her heart beating. It was unlikely that anyone would recognise her, she knew that, but still she felt a tug of fear at her heart. The houses were very like her own, small, brick terraced, back-to-back, but the signs on the walls were different. Long Live King Billy. Kick the Pope. No Surrender. When a child turned suddenly in front of her, she thought he was going to point his finger at her and shout. 'She's a Mick, come and get her!' . . . ❞ (A)*

*Across the Barricades* is a story in which ordinary people are hurt and even killed because of their religion. *Sectarian* violence like this has played a big part in Northern Ireland's recent history. What has been done to try and end this violence?

One night in July 1972 the army took down the barricades.

In 1973 the British Government and politicians in Northern Ireland agreed a method of sharing power between Protestants and Catholics. Many Nationalists like Bernadette McAliskey (formerly Devlin) did not think it would work:

❝ *This is deliberately meaningless. It is an attempt to con Nationalists into thinking they have gained a great victory and loyalists into believing they have lost nothing. This agreement is doomed.* ❞ (B)

Nevertheless, a Power Sharing Government was set up. However, in 1974 Unionists formed the United Unionist Council to organise strikes and disruptive activities to bring the Government down. Eamonn McCann recalled:

❝ *There were 12 hour electricity blackouts, a complete shutdown of gas supplies in some areas, no petrol, food shortages. In the countryside Protestant farmers blocked the roads with tractors and felled trees. Catholic workers who set out to march from the Bogside to the Maydown industrial estate were opposed by Loyalists as they tried to pass through the Waterside. The RUC baton-charged the Catholics.* ❞ (C)

In the same year the IRA began to bomb targets in Britain, to force the British public to take notice of the problems of Northern Ireland (see **D**). **E** shows an IRA car bomb exploding in London.

Sectarian violence continued in Ireland. On the night of 30 July 1975 members of a pop group, the *Miami Showband*, were ambushed as they were driving back to Dublin from Northern Ireland. The attackers also blew themselves up in the ambush:

❝ *40 yards away, near the still smouldering wreckage of the van, was an even more horrifying sight. In a pool of blood lay a mangled and burned hulk of human remains, with most of the head and brains blown away. A few yards from that were the entrails of what minutes earlier had been another man, now an even more unrecognisable heap . . . ❞ (F)*

*The Observer, January 1977*

Who were they?

❝ *For Detective Inspector Mitchell there was one immediate clue. A severed arm among the human remains had been tattooed with the letters 'UVF', which immediately identified the terrorists as being from the (Protestant) Ulster Volunteer Force. In any case within hours the 'Mid-Ulster branch of the UVF' issued a statement claiming responsibility.*

*Special Branch and Army Intelligence had for two months been fearing a major anti-Catholic terrorist operation by the UVF, ever since three Protestants had been murdered by the Provisional IRA at a fake road block . . . ❞ (G)*

The UVF attacked the *Miami Showband* because they thought it was an all-Catholic group. They did not realise that two of the members were Protestant.

Frightened and sick of the violence, what could the people of Northern Ireland do? Two women thought they had the answer. In 1976 Betty Williams and Mairead Corrigan formed *The Women's Peace Movement*:

❝ *The Belfast peace movement doubled in strength yesterday when at least 20 000 people flocked in warm sunshine to another rally at a park in east Belfast. The marchers led by a group of women from the Catholic Andersontown area of Belfast, defied threats from the Provisional IRA by parading with a 'Peace with Justice' banner through Protestant and mixed areas. Earlier Dr Ian Paisley's extremist Protestant newspaper the Protestant Telegraph added its voice to Provisional IRA attacks on the women's peace movement, describing it as 'spurious' (a sham) and 'priest-inspired' . . . ❞ (H)*

*The Observer, 22 August 1976*

## D  Table of Events 1972–77

**1972** *21 July* 'Bloody Friday'. Provisional IRA bombs in the centre of Belfast killed 9 civilians and injured more than 100.
*31 July* 'Operation Motorman'. Troops entered Catholic areas and removed the barricades.

**1973** *March* Two Provisional IRA car bombs exploded in London, 195 people were taken to hospital.
*August* IRA fire bombs went off in Harrods and other department stores in London's West End.
*December* 'The Sunningdale Agreement'. Moderate politicians in Northern Ireland agreed to power sharing.

**1974** *February* An IRA coach bomb on the M62 in England killed 12 people.
*March* Patrick Cosgrave, the Prime Minister of the Irish Republic, confirmed that his government accepted the existence of Northern Ireland as part of the UK.
*May* Ulster workers' strike brought down Brian Faulkner's power sharing government. Direct Rule was re-imposed.
*October* An IRA bomb in a Guildford pub killed 5 people and injured 6. Special powers were introduced for the arrest and detention of suspected terrorists in Britain.
*21 November* Two IRA pub bombings killed 21 people and injured 162.

**1975** *Winter* The IRA pub bombing campaign in Britain continued.
Another group – the Irish Republican Socialist Party – broke away from the Official IRA. Some of its members formed a military wing known as the Irish National Liberation Army.

**1976** *March* 'Special category' (political) status for terrorists in prison was ended.
*July* Christopher Ewart-Biggs, British Ambassador in Dublin, was blown up by a car bomb.
*August* Betty Williams and Mairead Corrigan founded the Women's Peace Movement.
*September* IRA prisoners protested against being refused political status by wearing only blankets instead of prison uniform.

E  Explosion of an IRA car bomb in London

## ??????????????

**1** Look at **A**.
**a** Why was Brede frightened to walk in the Protestant streets?
**b** What did the signs on the walls which said *'Long live King Billy'* and *'No surrender'* mean?
**c** Why were barricades put up in the streets of Northern Ireland?

**2 a** What is *sectarian* violence?
**b** What reason does **G** give for the sectarian murders in **F**?

**3** Explain why the attempt to share power between Catholics and Protestants failed in 1974.

**4** Why do you think both the Provisional IRA and Protestants like Ian Paisley criticised the Women's Peace Movement?

**5** Try to borrow copies of *Across the Barricades* by Joan Lingard, and *Under Goliath* by Peter Carter from your library. Write a short review of each book. Which do you think gives the clearest picture of life in Northern Ireland during the troubles?

# 31 Terror, Priests and Politicians

**A** The state funeral of Lord Mountbatten

The IRA campaign to make the British public 'sit up and take notice' took a new turn in 1979 when they killed a member of the British Royal Family. Lord Louis Mountbatten, Prince Charles' 'favourite uncle' was taking a fishing holiday at Mullaghmore, County Sligo, on the West coast of Ireland. The IRA planted a bomb on his boat and blew him up (**A**).

The IRA newspaper *An Phoblacht* made this statement:

*❛Execution of Soldier Mountbatten*
*In claiming responsibility for the execution of Lord Mountbatten (former Chief of the United Kingdom Defence Staff, cousin of the Queen of England and symbol of all that is imperial), the Irish Republican Army stated that the bombing was a 'discriminate (carefully chosen) operation to bring to the attention of the English people the continuing occupation of our country.*
*The British Army acknowledge that after ten years of war it cannot defeat us but yet the British Government continue with the oppression of our people and the torture of our comrades in the H-blocks (internment camps). Well, for this we will tear out their sentimental imperialist heart.'❜* (**B**)

*An Phoblacht, 1 September 1979*

How did the majority of Irish people feel about the use of violence?

The majority of Irish people are Catholics. In October 1979 there was great excitement when Pope John Paul II visited Southern Ireland (the Protestants would not let him visit the North). The Pope had this to say to all Irish people:

❛*Now I wish to speak to all men and women engaged in violence. I appeal to you, in language of passionate pleading. On my knees, I beg you, to turn away from the paths of violence and to return to the ways of peace. You may claim to seek justice, I too, believe in justice, and seek justice. But violence only delays the day of justice. Violence destroys the work of*

**D Table of Events January 1978 – May 1981**

| | |
|---|---|
| 1978 | *January* The European Court of Human Rights cleared Britain of using torture against internees but convicted Britain of 'inhuman and degrading' treatment of prisoners. |
| 1979 | *March* The Irish National Liberation Army assassinated Aiery Neave, the Conservative Party Spokesman on Northern Ireland.<br>*August* 10th anniversary of troops on the streets of Northern Ireland. The IRA assassinated Earl Mountbatten, a member of the Royal Family and killed 19 soldiers at Warren Point with booby-trap bombs.<br>*October* Pope John Paul II visited Southern Ireland and called for peace. |
| 1980 | *October–December* First hunger strike by IRA prisoners in Maze H-block prison to protest about not being given political status. |
| 1981 | *16 January* UDA attacked and seriously wounded Bernadette McAliskey (Devlin) and her husband, Michael, in their own home.<br>*6 February* Ian Paisley revived memories of the Unionists' resistance to Home Rule 1912–14.<br>He accused Margaret Thatcher and Charles Haughey (the Prime Ministers of Britain and the Irish Republic) of plotting to re-unite Ireland.<br>*1 March* IRA prisoners at the Maze Prison began a second hunger strike.<br>*9 April* Bobby Sands, leader of the IRA hunger strikers, was elected MP for Fermanagh in South Tyrone in a by-election.<br>*5 May* Bobby Sands was the first of the hunger strikers to die. His death sparked off riots and won worldwide publicity. |

*justice. Further violence in Ireland will only drag down to ruin the land you claim to love and the values you claim to cherish . . .'* (C)

Would the men and women of violence take any notice? Would this make the IRA change their tactics? Look at **D**. In 1981 IRA prisoners went on hunger strike because of the government's refusal to treat them as political prisoners (this right had been taken away in 1976). The government insisted that those found guilty of terrorism should be treated as ordinary criminals.

What did other countries think of the IRA hunger strike and the way the British Government handled it? Here are some comments from foreign newspapers:

*'The problem is deadlocked. The British Government is showing a serious lack of imagination by not seeing Ulster in any terms other than a police operation and maintaining law and order. A new political initiative is needed.*
Le Monde (France)

*They were considered terrorists, now they are martyrs.*
Die Arbeiter Zeitung (Vienna, Austria)

*You cannot help admiring a man who has the guts to die this way for a political aim.*
Ta Nea (Athens, Greece)

*The cruel tactics of a series of suicides has been successful . . .*
La Republica (Rome, Italy)

*The hunger strikers took the momentum away from the authorities. The IRA did that rather brilliantly, aided and abetted by a Prime Minister who doesn't seem to know the difference between 'no' and 'get lost'.*
Time Magazine (USA)

*We share the world's puzzlement that neither the British Government nor the people of Northern Ireland seem capable of bringing about a solution. We share the South African puzzlement that so many people in Britain can roundly condemn things in this country when far worse deeds are being perpetrated (done) in their own country.*
Die Transvaler (Johannesburg, South Africa)' (E)

**F** The funeral of hunger striker Tom McIlwee

**G** Cartoon in the *Sunday Express* newspaper, 17 May 1981

How accurate was their information? Compare **F** and **G**. **F** is a photograph taken at the funeral of one of the hunger strikers, Tom McIlwee. **G** shows what one British newspaper (the *Sunday Express*) thought of scenes like this.

Who was right, the foreign journalists or the *Sunday Express*? Would it have been better for the British Government to give in to the demands of the hunger strikers? What would have suited the IRA best?

# ??????????????????

**1** Look at **A**, **B** and **C**.
   **a** Why did the IRA decide to kill Lord Mountbatten?
   **b** Do you think the majority of Irish people are for or against the use of violence for political ends?

**2 a** Why did IRA prisoners go on hunger strike in 1981?
   **b** Do you think the British Government was right to treat the IRA prisoners as ordinary criminals?
   **c** What criticisms did foreign journalists make of Britain's handling of the hunger strike (**E**)?

**3** Look at photographs **A** and **F**. Why do you think the newspapers chose to print these pictures? How useful are such photographs to the historian?

**4** Using the evidence on these pages, and anything else you can find, discuss or write down your thoughts about one of the following statements:
   **a** *'Historians should not believe everything they read in newspapers or see on film about Northern Ireland'*
   **b** *'The media (newspapers, television etc) encourages the use of violence in Northern Ireland.'*

# 32 Solutions

Was there a solution to the continuing violence in Northern Ireland in 1984 (see **E**)? In 1981 Tony Benn, a British Labour MP said:

*'The present policy is a dead-end. There is no future for Ireland based on the presence of British troops. There has got to be a political initiative, and the way in which it has got to be done needs to be discussed. The tragedy is that we haven't had a proper discussion on Ireland. I think it was quite wrong to partition Ireland. I think it has proved wrong. Maybe the United Nations has got a role to play, with a peace-keeping force. But one thing is clear: the present policy has failed, is failing and will continue to fail. I should be content if we got a discussion going about how we could get British troops out and a solution in Ireland.'* (**A**)

Should British troops have been withdrawn? **B** shows how many Ulster people felt. Look at **C**. What does it suggest? Many people believed that if the army was withdrawn there would be a bloodbath – a civil war between the IRA and Protestant armies like the Ulster Defence Association. In 1982, 4045 houses were searched in Northern Ireland; 5066 lbs of explosives and 41 453 rounds of ammunition were found.

Was it possible for the Irish Nationalists to achieve what they wanted by peaceful methods? The deaths of the IRA hunger strikers in 1981 (see pages 60–61) increased sympathy and support for Provisional Sinn Fein, the political wing of the Provisional IRA. 42 per cent of Catholics living in Northern Ireland voted for

**B** Children protesting against the army presence in Northern Ireland

**C** Troop levels and violent deaths in Ulster

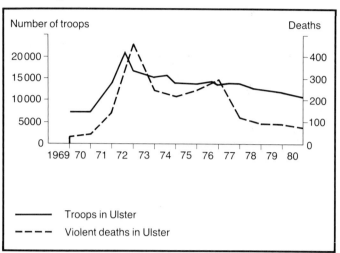

— Troops in Ulster
- - - Violent deaths in Ulster

Provisional Sinn Fein in the General Election of June 1983. Several Sinn Fein candidates were elected but refused to attend the British Parliament. History seemed to be repeating itself (see pages 32–33).

Look at **D**. In December 1983 the IRA once again struck at civilians in Britain. Provisional Sinn Fein leaders said that the IRA members who did this had acted against orders, and that they regretted what had happened. Were they sincere?

Did ideas like 'Rolling devolution' or 'The forum for a new Ireland' (see **E**) stand a chance of success? Can Nationalists and Unionists ever work together to bring peace to Ireland? In their own eyes, both sides in the 'troubles' of Ireland are in the right. What price must each side pay to live in peace?

## ???????????????

**1** Look at **A**, **B** and **D**.
  **a** Has the presence of the British army on the streets of Northern Ireland been a good or a bad thing? Why do you think so?
  **b** What do you think would happen if the troops were withdrawn?

**2** What has happened to ideas like 'Rolling devolution' and the 'Forum for a new Ireland'?

**3** Make a list of possible solutions to the deadlock in Northern Ireland. Give your reasons for and against each idea.

# HORROR AT *Harrods*—9 DEAD AS HUGE CAR BOMB ROCKS CAPITAL

**D** Newspaper headlines after the IRA car bomb explosion at Harrods

## E Timechart November 1981 – September 1985

**1981** *6 November* Britain and the Irish Republic agreed to set up an Anglo–Irish Council. This made Unionists like Paisley very suspicious.

*14 November* The IRA shot the Rev Robert Bradford, Unionist MP for Belfast South.

*23 November* The Rev Ian Paisley organised a Loyalist Day of Action by thousands of Protestants. Much of heavy industry was brought to a standstill.

**1982** *February–July* James Prior, Secretary of State for Northern Ireland, introduced a plan to restore self-rule (Rolling Devolution). An Assembly (Parliament) was to be elected by proportional representation. The rights of the Catholic minority would be protected.

*10 July* IRA bombs killed 10 soldiers in Hyde Park and Regents Park, London.

*20 October* Elections to the new Assembly were held. The moderate Nationalist party, the SDLP, refused to take part in these elections. Sinn Fein won 10% of the vote and six seats in the new Assembly.

*5 November* A United States court set free men known to be smuggling arms to the Provisional IRA.

*6 December* An Irish National Liberation Army bomb killed 17 people (11 of whom were British soldiers) in a bar in Ballykelly.

*8 December* The British Government banned the five Sinn Fein MPs elected to the new Northern Ireland Assembly from visiting Britain.

**1983** *31 January* The National Council for Civil Liberties launched a campaign against the use of plastic bullets.

*11 March* The Irish Republican Government invited all parties from Northern Ireland and Southern Ireland to join in a 'Forum for a New Ireland' to discuss a solution to the Irish Question.

*June* The British General Election was won by the Conservative Party. 42% of Catholics in Northern Ireland voted for Sinn Fein.

*25 September* 38 IRA prisoners escaped from Northern Ireland's 'top security' Maze Prison.

*12 November* Gerry Adams became the new President of Sinn Fein.

*21 November* The 'Official' Unionist Party withdrew from the new Northern Ireland Assembly after a violent attack on a Protestant church in Darkley, Co. Armagh.

*17 December* An IRA bomb outside the London department store Harrods killed 9 people.

**1984** *May* The report of the New Ireland Forum criticised the British Government over Northern Ireland and argued that Ireland could be united by peaceful means. James Prior (Secretary of State for Northern Ireland) said that he wished to resign.

*18 August* Serious rioting in the Protestant Shankhill district of Belfast, following arrest of 47 Protestants. They were tried for murder and membership of the Ulster Volunteer Force.

*10 September* Douglas Hurd replaced James Prior as Secretary of State for Northern Ireland.

*12 October* An IRA bomb at the Conservative Party Conference in Brighton killed five people.

**1985** *September* Tom King replaced Douglas Hurd as Secretary of State for Northern Ireland. *15 November* Anglo–Irish Agreement gave the Republican Government of Ireland a say in running Ulster despite fierce protest by Ulster Unionists.

# 33 The Future?

A

Look at **A**. It shows British soldiers charging up a street to deal with a riot. Children get involved in the riots, too – like the characters in the story *Across the Barricades*:

❝She leaned out further and saw that two soldiers were coming down the road. Then an arm was raised up and a brick went flying through the air.
'Trouble,' she cried quickly and ran from the room followed by Kate. Kate's mother was calling after them shouting to them to come back but they paid no attention. The children were all throwing stones now and anything else they could lay their hands on. One of the soldiers had a streak of blood on the side of his head . . .❞ (B)

Just a story? Look at photograph **C**, taken outside the Divis Flats, Belfast on 24 May 1981. Soldiers firing plastic bullets have dispersed rioters. This solitary boy advances challengingly. Only 25 yards away, he turns aside – to fight another day. Why do the children behave in this way?

❝'One, two, three, four, open up the H-Block door.' This is the nursery rhyme chanted by a three year old who lives near the Divis Flats in Catholic West Belfast. Running to the corner of the road, he spits at a crouching soldier. An eight year old girl, walking home from school in her uniform, picks up a stone to throw at a passing patrol. Toddlers make mini-barricades with dustbins and cardboard boxes . . .
. . . Children who are too young to understand seem filled with hatred. 'When soldiers put you in a Saracen, they beat your face with rifles,' said one. A mother said of her four year old: 'He throws stones – he enjoys it. If he sees a Saracen he dances and squeals and goes into a fit. If I manage to hold onto him, he screams at me that he's missed them. He wakes up in his cot in the morning shouting 'Gerry Fitt is a Brit'. All he

C

E

thinks of is soldiers, Brits and barricades.'❞ (D)

*The Sunday Times, 24 May 1981*

(Gerry Fitt is a Catholic politician who became unpopular with the Sinn Fein for being too moderate and for speaking out against the IRA.)

Now look at the boy leading the Orange March on 5 November in **E**. How old do you think he is?

Did the ideas of the 'Forum for a new Ireland' or the 1985 Anglo–Irish Agreement stand a chance of success?